Source Books on Education
Vol. 38

PROJECT
HEAD START

Garland Reference Library
of Social Science
Vol. 827

PROJECT HEAD START

Models and Strategies for the Twenty-First Century

Valora Washington
Ura Jean Oyemade Bailey

GARLAND PUBLISHING, Inc.
New York & London / 1995

Library of Congress Cataloging-in-Publication Data

Washington, Valora 1953–
    Project Head Start : models and strategies for the
twenty-first century / Valora Washington and Ura
Jean Oyemade Bailey.
        p.   cm. — (Garland reference library of social
science ; vol. 827. Source books on education ;
vol. 38)
    Includes bibliographical references (p.   ) and
indexes.
    ISBN 0–8153–0800–0. — ISBN 0–8153–1207–5
(pbk.)
    1. Project Head Start (U.S.)   2. Head Start pro-
grams—United States.   I. Bailey, Ura Jean Oyemade.
II. Title.   III. Series: Garland reference library of social
science ; v. 827.   IV. Series: Garland reference
library of social science. Source books on education ;
vol. 38.
LC4091.W36   1995
372.21'0973—dc20   94–36041
                                                      CIP

Paperback cover design by Patti Hefner

Printed on acid-free, 250-year-life paper
Manufactured in the United States of America

Dedicated to

Omari,

"the highest,"

and a wonderful assistant

and

Kamilah,

"the perfect one"

for our family,

even at two

Contents

Part B: Models and Strategies for the Twenty-First Century

Tables

Preface

When Ura Jean Oyemade and I wrote our first volume on Head Start in 1987, we had a sense that the needs of families in our society were changing rapidly and that Head Start services would need to respond to children and families in new ways. In the few years since that time, we have witnessed an explosion of challenges to Head Start effectiveness that was unimaginable when the program was designed in 1965. Chief among these challenges is the senseless violence that touches the lives of too many Head Start children, families, and communities. The threat of violence is closely coupled with rampant substance abuse. In both rural and urban communities, our children are growing up in the shadow of economic despair and nurtured by people of several generations who have been denied opportunities for the self-expression of their unique gifts and talents. All of us—and each of us—are diminished by these tragedies.

Yet in the midst of these communities are heroes and heroines, many of whom can be found as staff and volunteers in Head Start programs. These are the local community leaders, teachers, bus drivers, and social service coordinators committed to building children's dreams for a brighter future. With limited fiscal resources and great expectations, Head Start children are fed, clothed, housed, educated, and told clearly that they are valuable. The people doing the "telling" are generally themselves underpaid, public-assistance-eligible people who make great sacrifices because they care.

This book is a reference tool intended to celebrate the achievements of these heroes and heroines, while clarifying areas of program activity that can be strengthened and pointing the way for continued success in the twenty-first century.

My hope is that the leadership of our governments and private enterprises will begin to understand deeply the urgent need to invest in young children—that platitudes about the young are simply not enough. This book also aims to be a bridge of understanding, so that partnerships can emerge between the everyday heroes and the institutions of our nation.

Despite the academic tradition of objectivity, I boldly celebrate Head Start and salute the people who devote their daily lives to making it work. Yes, Project Head Start has serious flaws which I rush to recognize with the hope and expectation that they will be corrected. But in the context of our nation's development of the young, Head Start, although flawed, endures, thrives—even creates daily miracles. And these accomplishments are achieved with a program that is essentially experienced by the typical child on a limited, part-time basis for a single year. What else is our nation offering to these children?

I wish to express my gratitude to all of the people who have contributed to this work and to my life as this work was being prepared. Special tribute is given to my colleagues at the W.K. Kellogg Foundation, particularly the wise leadership of the president, Dr. Norman A. Brown. Special commendation is given to Sue Yoster, who guided this project in many ways. I also acknowledge Ura Jean Oyemade, with whom this work began in 1987. Finally, essential and invaluable support was provided by Carole Smith, Jean Kehoe, Valorie Johnson, Joyce Brown, and Carroll Green. Without their support very little of my work would be possible.

Valora Washington
Vice President—Programs
W.K. Kellogg Foundation
Battle Creek, Michigan

Abbreviations

ACYF	Administration on Children, Youth, and Families
AFDC	Aid to Families with Dependent Children
CDA	Child Development Associate
CDF	Children's Defense Fund
CDGM	Child Development Group of Mississippi
CED	Committee for Economic Development
CFRP	Child and Family Resource Program
FAS	Fetal Alcohol Syndrome
FY	Fiscal Year
GAO	General Accounting Office
GED	General Equivalency Diploma
GPO	Government Printing Office
HEW	U.S. Department of Health, Education, and Welfare
H.I.M.	Project Head Start Involving Males
JOBS	Job Opportunities and Basic Skills
JTPA	Jobs Training Partnership Act
MAT	Mathematics Achievement Test
NAEYC	National Association for the Education of Young Children
NAPARE	National Association for Perinatal Addiction Research and Education

NHSA	National Head Start Association
OCD	Office of Child Development
OEO	Office of Economic Opportunity
OHDS	U.S. Department of Education, Office of Human Development Services
OIG	Office of the Inspector General
OSAP	Office for Substance Abuse Prevention
OSPRI	On-Site Program Review Instrument
PCC	Parent and Child Centers
PCDC	Parent-Child Development Center
PET	Parent Effectiveness Training
RDE	Research, demonstration, and evaluation
SRS	Social Rehabilitation Service
T/TA	Training/Technical Assistance
HHS	U.S. Department of Health and Human Services
WIC	Special Supplemental Food Program for Women, Infants and Children

PART A

Moving Ahead with Head Start

CHAPTER 1

Project Head Start
A Paradox

Introduction

We must begin by acknowledging that Project Head Start is an enigma, a paradox.

On the one hand, "everybody loves Head Start" (Newsweek, Feb. 20, 1989). As we celebrate the twenty-ninth anniversary of Head Start, we see that 13 million children and their families have been served. For many of these people, Head Start offered hope and pointed a path to self-sufficiency, self-esteem and self-improvement.

In the aftermath of President Lyndon Johnson's "Great Society" programs, Head Start has not only survived but thrived, earning both bipartisan support and the adoration of community-based organizations. An article in *Fortune* magazine entitled "How We Can Win the War on Poverty" pointed to "the principle embodied in the federal Head Start Program" (Huey, 1989).

Head Start also enjoys the strong support of the U.S. public. Opinion surveys conducted for the Philip Morris Company and the Roosevelt Center for American Policy Studies indicate that the majority of Americans believe that Head Start should be expanded (NHSA, 1990). Head Start, then, has become "the long distance runner" (Dittmann, 1980), the "nation's pride" (NHSA, 1990), a "superstar" (Bollinger, 1981), an investment into our future, a program that has survived periods of budget cuts in other service programs and is often cited as an example of a successful federal program.

The National Head Start Association (1990) lists a wide array of organizations that support Head Start. These include the National Governors' Association, the National Conference of State Legislatures, the National Research Council, the Committee on Economic Development, and the National Alliance of Business.

Presidents of both major political parties have supported Head Start. President Jimmy Carter praised Head Start as "a program that works." President Ronald Reagan included Head Start in his "safety net" of social programs. President George Bush almost doubled Head Start funding. Right now, President Bill Clinton and Congress seem poised for massive expansions of the federal/local initiative, a move expected to create jobs, heighten awareness of the benefits of prevention over remediation, and enhance the lives of poor families throughout the United States.

Yet this vision of the "charmed life" of Head Start (Skerry, 1983), while undeniable, is only part of the story. Almost since its inception, Head Start has been haunted by persistent questions about its role in communities, its sustainable impacts, and its quality. Challenged to produce evidence of the intellectual and social gains children have made over time, Head Start advocates over the decades have repeatedly scrambled to articulate answers to politicians and the public who expected "more." Right now, even long-time friends of the project, notably Dr. Edward Zigler, have publicly criticized the uneven quality of Head Start programs. Also, some Head Start directors have worried that their long-time dream of "serving every eligible child" could turn into a nightmare given a too rapid pace of proposed expansions. Furthermore, as Head Start services in 1994 are offered in a broader and more complex array of child care and early education programs than existed in 1965, there are clear tensions related to "coordination"—including competition for fiscal resources—and questions about the capacity or willingness of other types of educare to serve poor children, especially children of color.

Contrasting Images of Head Start

As long-time observers of the Head Start paradox, we are struck by how little is actually known about Head Start, given its twenty-nine year history and the vast quantity of opinion and editorials devoted to the subject. It is not our intent to defend Head Start against the many legitimate criticisms and varied perceptions. While these criticisms and perceptions are controversial and not necessarily verified by empirical investigation, they are important to consider in discussions of how best to "move ahead with Head Start." Here are some of the major concerns that have been expressed about Project Head Start:

- The existing infrastructure of Head Start has weakened considerably over the years at multiple levels, such as managerial and facility capacities (HHS, 1980; NHSA, 1990).

- The effectiveness of Head Start services, which ostensibly enjoy a "safety net," has been severely impacted by the elimination of, or budget and staff reductions in, other federal programs on which Head Start depends (CDF, 1985; Washington and Oyemade, 1987). For example, a Minnesota state preschool screening program, which no longer exists, paid for health screenings for Head Start children (CDF, 1983A and 1983B).

- Today, 55 percent of Head Start children live with a single parent, often a very young mother (CDF, 1993). In this environment, many Head Start programs are ill-equipped to address the challenges posed by changing family trends or by social problems such as substance abuse, violence, teenage pregnancy, and illiteracy. The Central Vermont Head Start/Family Foundations program reported, for example, that one-third to two-thirds of its families had substance abuse problems in the home, that 40 percent of its mothers had their first children as teenagers, and that 32 percent of the parents had no high school diploma or GED (Besharov, 1992b).

Douglas Besharov (1992B) states, "the Head Start manual does not say what to do when the staff finds a decapitated body on the playground, or when a group of four-year-olds finds a pile of used hyperdermic needles and starts sticking each other with them. But it should because in any high-poverty area in the country you can hear similar stories from the staff of preschool programs."

- "One out of every five preschool children is affected in some way by substance abuse," according to a Head Start handbook for grantees (Collins and Anderson, 1991, p. 3). "It is reasonable to assume that adults associated with Head Start may be affected by substance abuse in the same proportion as the general adult population."

- Among 5,000 families in one demonstration preschool program, five, and perhaps six, mothers died violent deaths in less than a year—seventeen times the violent death rate for women fifteen to twenty-four in the population as a whole (Besharov, 1992B). The violence goes both ways; one mother shot the caseworker assigned to her preschooler's class because the worker was allegedly dating the mother's boyfriend.

- Head Start is not immune to the challenges generally faced in the early childhood field—high staff turnovers and low wages. Besharov (1992B) argues that many Head Start programs are "child care ghettos for low-income mothers who collect Aid to Families with Dependent Children"; 68 percent of all Head Start children are on AFDC, a figure that has climbed steadily over the years.

- There is some concern that Head Start is a second-class citizen in a field it helped to stimulate: individuals who receive child development training, certification, and even academic degrees through Head Start are often lured to better-financed, higher status roles in institutions like public schools that typically offer better pay, benefits, and working conditions.

Building on Head Start Strengths

These and other very poignant challenges within Head Start programs must be understood in view of a very critical fact: The Head Start program is still the federal government's largest source of direct support for early childhood services for children of low-income families, although only a fraction of eligible children are currently served by the program. In addition, Head Start is a major vehicle for the provision of federal leadership for all types of early childhood services through its research and development activities, innovative projects, and the provision of training and technical assistance.

Moreover, there are many excellent Head Start programs throughout the nation: A recent study by the U.S. Department of Education (Layzer, Goodson and Moss, 1993) found that Head Start programs were more likely than other early childhood programs to provide comprehensive services such as health care and nutritious meals, and to involve parents in their childrens' learning. The study also reported that Head Start programs are more likely to meet national accreditation standards for good quality programs than many other early childhood and child care programs.

Moreover, Head Start has been a role model of preschool programs with respect to diversity issues. Many Head Start practitioners believe that the early childhood field is dominated by middle- and upper-middle-class practitioners and researchers who cannot—or will not—serve or recognize the aspirations of low-income, racially and ethnically diverse Head Start communities.

For these reasons alone, we agree with the "Scholars' Letter to Congress" (1993) and the Children's Defense Fund (1993B) that the fact that some Head Start programs need improvement cannot and should not be used as an excuse for "delaying, whittling down, or opposing" Head Start expansion.

More Than Preschool Education: Head Start
Offers Something for Everyone

These contrasting images of Head Start—as early childhood innovator and national disappointment—are largely due to the "naive environmentalism" that created Head Start and that persists in judgments about its effectiveness. Very quickly in the 1960s, both the press and public grasped the value of Head Start as a preschool education program with the potential to erase the gaps in the academic performance of poor and middle-class children. Indeed, Head Start induced disappointment and criticism as scientists reported that the immediate cognitive gains of Head Start children "fade out" and do not persist over time.

Yet Head Start has *always* been designed to be more than preschool education. In the past twenty-nine years, Head Start has provided millions of children with health care, nutritious meals, and social services. Head Start has helped parents to be more involved in their children's learning and to become more self-sufficient.

The multiple goals of Project Head Start are built into its very fabric, yet have always been at the core of the tremendous challenges which Head Start faces. We are not the first to observe that much of Head Start's resilience may actually be credited to the confusion about its goals, as well as the fact that it has multiple goals. Head Start offers something for everyone and thereby garners a wide spectrum of supporters:

- For community activists, Head Start demonstrates the value of local control.

- For early childhood educators, Head Start develops and nurtures the young.

- For "family support" and "family values" promoters, Head Start emphasizes parent involvement with their children and with those institutions that affect the children's lives.

- For health care providers, Head Start offers children nutritious meals, immunizations, and mandates screening/diagnosis/treatment for every child.

- To the welfare reform strategist, Head Start offers jobs for parents, as well as job training, child care enabling parents to work, and a focus on economic self-sufficiency.

- To those who seek stronger coordination of social services and "one-stop shopping," Head Start since 1965 has helped social services agencies to be more responsive to the poor, while promoting cooperation among agencies.

- Head Start was a strong forerunner to "Goal One" of the national education goals: "By the year 2000, every child will be ready to learn." Emphasizing preschool education and social competence skills, Head Start has undeniably produced immediate gains for children upon school entry.

It's Not a Chameleon

Some critics claim that the nonacademic goals of Head Start serve to "cover up" the negative press of the fade-out theory on Head Start's effectiveness. In this sense, Head Start might be viewed as a chameleon that adjusts to and defines itself through evolving social nuances. We suggest that any objective student of Head Start quickly realizes that the goals of Head Start have always been multiple—therein lies its programmatic strength and the challenge of articulating its effectiveness.

CHAPTER 2

Celebrating Head Start

Head Start: A Forerunner of Today's Vision for Children

Without ignoring the serious challenges which have faced and continue to face Head Start, there is a clear need to develop a broader understanding of Head Start's accomplishments. Project Head Start has been a trailblazer that has helped to focus tremendous public attention on the needs of young children that currently exist. As we celebrate Head Start's victories for children, it is highly appropriate for the Head Start community of parents, staff, and volunteers to recognize the important role that they have played as leaders who helped to make all of these victories possible. For twenty-nine years, Head Start children, parents, volunteers, and staff have been demonstrating their conviction in the power of early childhood and have consistently articulated a vision of comprehensive services for children.

Five Million Children

We are constantly reminded that our children need and deserve so much more than we as a society have yet given to them. While the number of *poor people* in the United States has been relatively stable over the last twenty years, the number of *poor children* under age six has increased significantly. In 1991, there were 5.6 million children under the age of six living in poverty in the United States. That is nearly one out of every four babies, toddlers, and preschoolers (National Center for Children in Poverty, 1993).

Yet there are converging signs of social change for children:

- It is becoming increasingly clear to the average American that efforts to enhance the social, intellectual, and physical development of children must begin early in their lives.

- Laws for young children, like Public Law 99-457, overwhelmingly affirmed what the Head Start community has practiced for a long time: families must be empowered, and parents and professionals must function in a collaborative fashion.

- There is a diverse array of support for "full funding of Head Start," although the definition of "full funding" may vary.

- State and local spending on early childhood programs continues to increase: whereas only seven states funded their own pre-kindergarten programs in 1980, over thirty states do so today (Advisory Committee on Head Start Quality and Expansion, 1993).

Even in the midst of the great strides that we have taken for children in recent years, it is still true that there is little in U.S. social policy, aside from the public school, which matches political rhetoric to the actual resources we need for children and families. Indeed, care for children, and family support, have generally been considered private matters that families are supposed to take care of as best they can. Project Head Start is a notable exception to our national public response to children.

Why We Celebrate Project Head Start

As Project Head Start celebrates its twenty-ninth year, it is clearly recognized as one of the most successful and enduring antipoverty programs in the United States. It was started as a demonstration to determine whether the cycle of poverty could be interrupted through a focus on families with young children. Over the past twenty-nine years, Head Start has advanced far beyond the original experimental demonstration stage. Even as we recognize the critical need for improvements in Head Start, there are many reasons why the program continues to generate excitement and commitment.

- First, Head Start is important because of its impact on children. Head Start helps kids get better.
- Second, Head Start has demonstrated its capacity to empower parents and communities.
- Third, Head Start has led the way in demonstrating new models for the field of early childhood education.
- Fourth, Head Start has been the leader in helping our nation to face and to overcome its contradictions about children.

Because of Its Impact on Children

It is impossible to describe the power of Head Start without thinking of the 13 million children who have been served since 1965.

The impressive and immediate gains for children served by Head Start have been well documented, particularly in terms of educational achievement and in building the social competence necessary to help children become more effective in their everyday environments of home, school, and community. Noting these immediate benefits, Head Start advocates are understandably dismayed when project effectiveness is judged on the basis of whether the impact "fades out" after three or four years.

Zigler (1973, p.372) argues that, "Besides being erroneous, the worst hangover of the fade-out position is that it provides ammunition to those in America who feel that expending money in an effort to improve the lives of economically disadvantaged children is a waste." Many Head Start advocates bluntly assert that if some kids do not keep the Head Start advantages by the time they are in second or third grade, then maybe we ought to look at how elementary schools can better continue the successes begun in the preschool years.

Head Start cannot "inoculate" children against the bitter ravages of poverty, especially since the Head Start experience for any given child is typically part time over one single year! But Head Start does indeed work miracles in the face of poverty and funding limitations.

- Head Start studies are virtually unanimous in finding that Head Start has immediate positive effects on children's cognitive ability.

- Head Start appears to affect the long-term school achievement of participants. Children in Head Start are less likely to have to repeat a grade or to be put in special education classes.

- Children who attend Head Start benefit immediately in terms of their self-esteem, achievement/motivation, and social behavior.

- Head Start studies have found that Head Start has a positive effect on child health, motor development, nutrition, and dental care.

- If for no other reason, Head Start should be celebrated as a successful model of health care to young children. In many communities, Head Start plays a major role in providing and coordinating local social and health services for disadvantaged families. Several reviews have been compiled on the health component of Head Start and health outcomes (for examples, see Ellsworth Associates, 1993; Hale, Seitz, and Zigler, 1990; also see Meisels, 1988; Thacker, Addis, and Goodman, 1992; Hall, 1992). According to the HHS (1990) in 1988–89:

  - Ninety-nine percent of Head Start kids complete medical screening if they are enrolled at least ninety days;

  - If a problem is found, 98 percent of Head Start kids needing treatment receive it;

  - Ninety-eight percent of children completed all required immunizations; and

- Ninety-five percent of Head Start families received social services directly from Head Start or through referral to other agencies.

These child health results are victories achieved in Head Start that are not achieved for other poor children.

Because It Empowers Parents and Communities

For parents, Head Start has offered career training and employment—about 30 percent of staff members are former or current Head Start parents, and many of these parents are among the 45 percent of staff members who have earned early childhood degrees or the Child Development Associate (CDA) credential. As a result of Head Start's strong emphasis on parent involvement, many Head Start parents begin to view themselves as the primary educators of and decision makers for their children.

Study after study has shown high parental approval of Project Head Start. A recent survey by the National Head Start Association (1990) found that parents expressed a high level of program satisfaction: 90 percent of the parents spontaneously indicated a positive effect on their child, such as on the child's education, social skills, self-sufficiency, self-discipline, health/ nutrition, motivation to learn, self-confidence, and speech. Many parents also reported improvement in the parent-child relationship by helping the parent to better understand or teach the child and helping the family to learn together, communicate better, feel closer to each other, spend more time together, and feel proud of the child. NHSA correctly points out that it is rare to see such a high degree of satisfaction among the participants in a social program.

One way that parents show their support is by their active participation with their children in Head Start. For example, in 1992, more than 950,000 parents volunteered in their local Head Start programs (HHS, Project Head Start Statistical Fact Sheet, 1993). When parents are involved with Head Start, it may be that gains for children are more likely to be maintained. Yet it is surprising how relatively little research has been conducted in the area of parent involvement. For example, a recent meta-analysis conducted by White, Taylor, and Moss (1992) concluded that there is no convincing evidence that the ways in which parents have been involved in previous early intervention research studies result in more effective outcomes.

Evaluations of the impact of the parent involvement component of the program are rather limited and largely anecdotal. The stories about parent involvement have been as varied as the character of the parent involvement component of the Head Start program. For example, in New York City, a group of fathers of Head Start children got together and decided that what they needed were jobs. They studied together to take the examination to be sanitation engineers in New York City. They got the manuals, studied, passed the examination, and started getting jobs (see Washington and Oyemade, 1987).

Head Start alumni—both children and parents—have attended and graduated from many universities. Parent involvement can encourage both children and parents to earn academic credentials. The case of "Loretta" highlights how one individual can benefit from parent involvement in Head Start. A high school dropout who was working in a snack bar at a college, Loretta's involvement in her daughter's Head Start program led to further work toward her GED and ultimately to enrollment in college, where she graduated with a degree in human services. She was later employed as the Head Start social services/parent involvement coordinator for her local community action agency.

But the benefits of parent involvement can extend beyond personal growth for individuals. Perhaps another under-recognized value of Project Head Start is its favorable impact on local communities. By providing jobs and services in 2,000 communities across the country, Head Start has been demonstrated to increase the involvement of the poor in public decision making, increase employment of the poor as paraprofessionals, encourage communities to put more emphasis on the educational needs of the poor, and lead to the modification of health services and practices to serve the poor better and more sensitively.

In sum, Head Start can effectively make local institutions more responsive to the poor. The case of a Head Start program in the mountains of central Pennsylvania is illustrative of parent involvement seen as "community change." These communities could not get TV reception. Eight members of the local Head Start policy committee arranged to have a cable system installed in the two communities. Parent involvement helped these families to realize that they could have an impact on their environment (Washington and Oyemade, 1987).

Another example of Head Start promoting community change was the Head Start program operated by the Child Development Group of Mississippi (CDGM). With an emphasis on the fullest participation by recipients, each of the eighty-four centers was run by a local committee of poor people, which was responsible for the planning, program hiring, administration, and, ultimately, the success or failure of the center. Through this program, many of the parents, such as Fannie Lou Hamer, became formidable political figures (Washington and Oyemade, 1987).

Perhaps the development of leadership potential among the poor, as a consequence of parental participation in Head Start, is an important factor in optimizing children's development. The question raised is whether a child's sense of control is affected by the leadership behavior modeled by the children's parents. When kids see their parents as powerful and proactive members of society, the kids may also get the idea that they can influence their own destiny.

Because It Has Led the Way in Demonstrating New Models for the Fields of Child Development and Early Childhood Education

Head Start has supported a variety of demonstration projects to encourage communities to create and implement innovative ways of addressing the needs of low-income families with young children. For children with a parent behind bars, for families without homes, for families who are experiencing rejection and isolation because a child has AIDS—in these and other instances, many Head Start programs are taking the lead in coordinating and improving services and trying to enhance the quality of life for Head Start families.

The 1990s have ushered in an era characterized by certain watchwords that have always been heard within Head Start. The search is now for "comprehensive," "collaborative" programs which will "reinvent government" (Osborne and Gaebler, 1992). Perhaps this will facilitate broader understanding that Head Start is much more than a preschool program.

For example, from the beginning, Head Start has been committed to forming relationships with other agencies that share the goal of family self-sufficiency. Like many service providers, Head Start is encountering increasing numbers of families affected by substance abuse, chronic unemployment or underemployment, and low literacy skills. These critical and often interrelated problems disrupt efforts to help families become self-sufficient. Given the complexity of these problems, it is clear that neither Head Start nor any single family service agency can be effective working alone.

During the past twenty-nine years, Head Start has served as a national laboratory for innovative early childhood services. As described in Chapters 4 through 7 of this book, Head Start launched a series of national demonstration projects to test new ways to serve kids.

Head Start has grown more effective over the years, partly as a result of these improvements and innovations. Research indicates that the impact of Head Start on children's intellectual development was roughly twice as great after 1970 as in 1969 and corresponds to the period in which several important improvements were introduced into Head Start. It is clear that effective program strategies can upgrade program quality. We celebrate Head Start because it has led the way.

Because It Has Been the Leader in Helping Our Nation Face and Overcome Its Contradictions About Children

Those who have watched the program over the years know that the current public resurgence of confidence in Project Head Start is something many communities have worked hard to earn—and it hasn't always been this way. In the early years, in the South, some local whites found it difficult to accept Head Start because of the idea of self-determination and management by local black people. Others, such as Senator John Stennis, alleged that Head Start in Mississippi consisted of "out of state" civil rights activists who used program funds for civil rights and other unauthorized activities (Washington and Oyemade, 1987).

But now Head Start is so popular that it is being widely imitated. Numerous programs claim to be "Head Start-like." Today at least thirty-five states have state-funded preschool programs. Several states supplement Head Start funds or use a Head Start model. Other state programs, however, lack the scope of services provided by Head Start (Mitchell, Seligson and Marx, 1989). Polly Greenberg of NAEYC reminds us that if it is not part of an antipoverty program that makes every effort to help enrollees' families do better economically, it is not a genuine, high-quality Head Start program nor is it a true "Head Start-like" program (Greenberg, 1990).

When we summarize the victories of Head Start, we can point to children who are better prepared for school and who can perform at higher levels once they are in school. But we can also point with pride at the broader range of Head Start effects— effects on child and family health and nutrition, parent-child relations, parental self-esteem, self-sufficiency, and community development.

In a nation that is generally unsure about the direction it wants to go with children—and with education—Head Start is celebrated for playing an important part in helping our nation to realize its investment in children.

Today, unlike 1965, there are more early childhood programs funded through a combination of local, state, and federal public and private sector funds; new welfare reform initiatives continue to further expand the range, variety, and demand for full-day early childhood services (NHSA, 1990). Yet we must remember that despite program growth, low-income children today are less likely to be enrolled in pre-primary programs than non-low-income children; while the number of poor preschool-age children has increased, most are not in preschool (GAO, 1993).

CHAPTER 3

A Head Start Primer

To understand the context in which our nation can "move ahead with Head Start," we begin with a brief history of the project, including its administrative structure and current status.

History

In the early 1960s, U.S. citizens and the Kennedy administration rediscovered what Michael Harrington labeled "the other America," in which it was estimated that nearly one-quarter of the American people lived in poverty. The impoverished lacked adequate food, housing, and health care, and their isolation from the mainstream of American culture had an equally devastating but less obvious effect on their economic status (Harrington, 1962).

In response to this concern, President Kennedy suggested that "the prevention of adult poverty and dependency must begin with the case of dependent children." This concept was based on the "culture-of-poverty" notion that poverty and welfare dependencies are transmitted intergenerationally largely because values and motivations deemed vital to economic achievement—education, independence, ambition, concern for the future—are not reinforced during a childhood spent in poverty and dependence on welfare (Hill and Ponza, 1983).

Based on this view, the Economic Opportunity Act of 1964 created the Office of Economic Opportunity (OEO), which was the major weapon in an "unconditional war on poverty." President Johnson declared a war "not only to relieve the symptoms of poverty but to cure it; and, above all, to prevent it." Although the legislation did not mandate Head Start or any similar program, it did direct OEO to pay special attention to the needs of young people (Zigler and Anderson, 1979).

Research and public policy coincided to create the impetus for the development of the Head Start program. Two classic volumes were influential in redirecting empirical thought about child development. In the first, J. McVicker Hunt's *Intelligence and Experience*, published in 1961, concluded that experience programs the development of the human brain and affects the rate of early development in human infants. In 1964, Benjamin Bloom's classic work, *Stability and Change in Human Characteristics*, concluded that important human characteristics showed a pattern of very rapid growth in the early years and then steadily declined. For general intelligence, Bloom surmised that about 50 percent of the variation possible for any particular child was established by age four. In sharp contrast to belief in predetermined and fixed development, Bloom's work set the stage for a decade of vigorous insistence of the predominant role of the environment in development. Moreover, since the environment can be adjusted, Bloom willingly addressed himself to the question of social responsibility for disadvantaged children (Steiner, 1976).

However, these volumes did not directly translate into public policy. Rather, Steiner suggests that, whatever their importance for later efforts to effect social change, the short-run importance of these books was the coincidence of their timing with the political needs and purposes of the Kennedy and Johnson presidencies. President Kennedy's original antipoverty task force did not pinpoint preschool children in the proposed community action program. Indeed, Head Start was not invented until six months after enactment of the Economic Opportunity Act, presumably with the hope of developing a more comprehensive program that would show quick results (Steiner, 1976).

Head Start was proposed by an interdisciplinary panel chaired by Dr. Robert E. Cooke, professor of pediatrics at Johns Hopkins University School of Medicine, a man with close ties to the Kennedy family. The panel, charged with considering the kinds of programs potentially effective to increase achievement and opportunities for the poor, targeted the preschool population for assistance. The panel recommended that the preschool effort be comprehensive, including health, education, and social services, to compensate for the children's lack of the kinds of experiences and opportunities available to economically advantaged families (Steiner, 1976).

As part of the OEO efforts to implement the community action provision of the act, Head Start was suggested as a program that would be "a microcosm of community action." It would offer major advantages beyond the services it would provide to children and their families. It would have a visible emotional impact as a symbol of OEO's potential. The program would fulfill community action obligations by involving parents in planning the centers. Parents and youth could also obtain jobs as aides. Shriver hoped that Head Start would "bring together all of the different resources within different local agencies on one target—the child that is poor, and his family" (Ross, 1979).

The special importance of Head Start was said to be its provision of a unique range of services. It combined day care with medical and dental treatment, emphasized both the child's psychological development and school readiness, and introduced "social services into the child's home environment, plus education of the parents" (Ross, 1979).

Steiner (1976) concluded that the preexistence of the antipoverty program provided the environment for creating Head Start. Once in place, the project expanded interest in early childhood. Child development experts, Steiner adds, too readily acquiesced as Head Start moved from experiment to institution without wide-ranging debate about likely costs, benefits, or alternatives. Only after evaluation studies questioned the investment value of Head Start (Cole and Washington, 1986) did many Head Start planners speak publicly about "the naive environmentalism which caused Head Start to be oversold in the early days" (Steiner, 1976, p. 29).

Thus, Project Head Start was launched during the summer of 1965 with the expectation of spending about $17 million for about 100,000 children. However, the demand was far greater than anticipated due largely to the massive manner in which the program was advertised. As a result, the Office of Economic

Opportunity decided to support a much larger program than originally planned, despite the Cooke panel's warning that it would be preferable to have comprehensive programs for fewer children than to reach vast numbers of children with limited programs. Finally, 561,359 children were enrolled in 11,068 centers in the summer of 1965.

Head Start was extremely popular, in contrast with some of the OEO's other programs (Steiner, 1976). Steiner asserts that Head Start achieved its instant and continuing popularity by focusing essentially on one model of service—organized centers serving preschool children. This focus was adopted as a matter of administrative policy, not of statute. The Economic Opportunity Act of 1964, and the subsequent amendments to it which wrote a Head Start program into law, anticipated maximum community group freedom in choosing services such as prenatal care, child development training for parents, and in-home services. However, the amassing strength of the program made it quickly apparent that it would be difficult to alter the program either by administrative action or by statutory authorization for alternative models—even in the face of early evidence which cast doubt on the model's effectiveness on cognitive development. Throughout the Johnson administration, however, the value of Head Start as an effective instrument of early education was widely accepted by the public, by Congress, and by social scientists (Zigler and Muenchow, 1992).

However, by 1969, during the administration of President Richard Nixon, a massive evaluation of Head Start by Westinghouse Learning Corporation began to raise important questions about the lasting benefits of Head Start. Of the nine major findings of the Westinghouse report, the most positive dealt with parents' strong approval of the program and its effect on their children.

Response to the Westinghouse report was mixed, far-reaching, and controversial. President Nixon's planned strong endorsement of Project Head Start was transformed into an ambiguous statement describing the effort as still "experimental" (Steiner, 1976).

Edward Zigler says that the negative impact of the Westinghouse report was so powerful that his first job on taking over Head Start in 1970 was to fight to keep the program alive (Zigler and Rescorla, 1985). The program was still on a tentative footing when the "fade-out" assessment of Head Start outcomes was widely proclaimed by 1975. From 1975 to 1978, several national media sources reported that Head Start had been terminated, as the program faded from view (Zigler and Rescorla, 1985).

Nevertheless, Head Start was staunchly defended, and it remained popular among participants and acceptable to Congress. Presently, Head Start is enjoying a resurgence in public confidence. In fact, recent congressional action to expand the program suggests that it has regained its favored position of the past. The present status is no doubt largely due to the fact that credible program data and favorable evaluation studies about preschool education are now available and widely publicized (e.g., Berruetta-Clement et al., 1984; Schweinhart and Weikart, 1993). The project is widely acclaimed by members of both major political parties. Importantly, the project maintains wide popularity in local communities.

Edward Zigler's (1979) observation about Head Start is quite clear: Head Start is less a static program than an evolving concept constantly in need of evaluation. Zigler lists five forces that kept Head Start alive in the 1980s during a Republican administration. These factors are also critical to continuing support in the 1990s:

1. Effective support by parents, staff, and advocacy groups such as the Children's Defense Fund;
2. A positive image in the media;
3. Strong bipartisan congressional support;
4. Robust, reliable research demonstrating the long-term cost-effective benefits of Head Start; and
5. Powerful converts to the program who, after working with Head Start, have become advocates—a sequence of events which Zigler notes is quite common (Zigler, 1985).

Administration

Although the political and policy status of Head Start changes, since 1965, the program's goals have remained virtually unchanged. The program's administration and operating structure, however, have been modified over time.

Decision-making in Head Start is shaped at several administrative levels including the federal Head Start agency, regional offices, and local grantees and delegate agencies. In the next few pages, the role of each of these units in the administrative structure is discussed, and the Head Start funding mechanism is described.

The Federal Head Start Agency

As one of the programs funded by the Economic Opportunity Act of 1964, Project Head Start was initially administered by the Office of Economic Opportunity (OEO) created by the act. At that time, the director of Head Start was not subject to congressional confirmation. The intent of the legislation was that Head Start would be located in OEO only until it demonstrated its workability and effectiveness, at which time, like other OEO programs, it would be transferred to an unspecified cabinet department.

By 1968, however, concern about combining community action with preschool education and child care led to a directive from the president to study the feasibility of moving Head Start from OEO to another government agency. A month after his inauguration, President Nixon announced his intention to delegate the operation of Head Start to the U.S. Department of Health, Education, and Welfare (HEW), although he did not specify which office in HEW. As Richard Nixon began his presidency, there were also perceptions that, while OEO was facing an uncertain future, HEW was on the upswing.

Faced with a choice of offices within HEW, there was little enthusiasm for the prevailing three options: the Office of Education, the Children's Bureau, and the Social Rehabilitation Service (SRS). There were misgivings about the involvement of professional educators, and concern that SRS's preoccupation with public assistance and work training programs would overshadow child development considerations. An obvious logical possibility was the Children's Bureau, which staffed social work concerns such as foster care and adoption services. However, the Bureau—perceived as traditional, maternalistic, nonaggressive, non-innovative, and out of touch with the issues of poor and black children—discouraged child development activists of the 1960s from using it as a focal point for an expanded program of federal intervention in early childhood.

Consequently, the decision was made to delegate Head Start to a new agency of HEW: an Office of Child Development (OCD) was endowed with "high prestige and visibility" as it became the focal point of new initiatives in both child development and programs it acquired from the Children's Bureau. Edward Zigler, a Yale University psychologist, served as OCD's first director, a position he held for two years. By this time, the growth of Head Start had come to an end as the number of individual projects, enrollment totals in full year programs, and federal appropriations stabilized. However, increasingly less sure of the national administration's commitment to children, Zigler tried to innovate by encouraging the idea of a credential for beginning professionals or "child development associates," and by varying the Head Start service delivery model. Nevertheless, OCD was, in the final analysis, degraded in the HEW hierarchy; its new responsibilities were limited to making grants to combat child abuse. According to Steiner (1976), OCD proved to have no more political influence than the old Children's Bureau.

In 1977, OCD became the Agency for Children, Youth and Families (ACYF). Today, Head Start is administered by the Adminstration on Children, Youth, and Families, currently a part of the Office of Human Development Services in the U.S. Department of Health and Human Services (HHS).

Regional Offices

Grants are awarded by the HHS regional offices and the Indian and Migrant Program Division to local public agencies, private nonprofit organizations, and school systems for the purpose of operating Head Start programs at the community level. Head Start funding is provided competitively to "grantees" (public or private nonprofit organizations) to carry on all or part of the work.

Within Head Start, as in most federal grant programs, field administration is decentralized into ten regional headquarter cities. Conceptually, regional office responsibilities have traditionally consisted of developing and processing grants, monitoring grantee operations, and providing technical support to local grantees. Each region has a core staff of program specialists and a team of community representatives who oversee and support the activities of local Head Start grantees.

Grantees

Grantees—the public or private nonprofit agencies granted assistance by the federal government to carry on individual Head Start programs—by law have responsibility for the actual operation of Head Start programs. It is federal policy to continue to leave the responsibility for Head Start with an existing grantee so long as it remains "viable" and conforms to Head Start performance standards (Harmon and Hanley, 1979). Thus, barring major expansion of Project Head Start, there is little change in the composition of the grantee network.

Delegate Agencies

While grantees can and do operate Head Start programs directly, they often delegate some or all of the operational responsibility to other organizations. These organizations, known as "delegate agencies," are public or private nonprofit associations. Thus, while there is a single Head Start policy, there are more than 2,000 locally administered Head Start programs of varying quality. Head Start remains essentially a collection of locally run, autonomous programs.

Head Start Program Goals, Component Areas, and Performance Standards

According to the Head Start performance standards:

> The overall goal of Head Start is to bring about a greater degree of social competence in the children of low-income families. By social competence is meant the child's everyday effectiveness in dealing with both the present environment and later responsibilities in school and life.

To achieve this goal, Head Start is designed to:

1. Improve the child's physical health and physical abilities.
2. Help the emotional and social development of the child by encouraging self-confidence, spontaneity, curiosity, and self-discipline.
3. Improve the child's mental processes and skills, with particular attention to conceptual and verbal skills.
4. Establish patterns and expectations of success for the child that will create a climate of confidence for future learning efforts.
5. Increase the child's capacity to relate positively to family members and others, while at the same time strengthening the family's ability to relate positively to the child.
6. Develop in the child and the family a responsible attitude toward society, and encourage society to work with the poor in solving their problems.
7. Increase the sense of dignity and self-worth within the child and the family (Richmond, Stipek, and Zigler, 1979).

The goals of Head Start are related to four component areas around which grantees devise their programs: educational services, health services, social services, and parent involvement.

It should be noted that in the early years of Head Start, the project was reluctant to issue specific program guidelines except in areas like parent participation and career development (policy

documents in these areas were seen as necessary to force
compliance by the public school delegate agencies). This reluc-
tance, Harmon and Hanley (1979) point out, was out of respect
for "local control" and the notion that the programs were
accountable primarily to parents, except in matters of fiscal
integrity. Thus, as late as 1970, Head Start administrators did not
have accurate data as to how many children were served or what
services were actually provided at what cost or benefit.

However, as a result of criticisms fueled by the Westinghouse report and the development of Head Start as a large, fairly
stable program that could no longer be excused for uneven
performance, broad programs of management and programmatic reform were initiated. Chief among these reforms was the
development and promulgation of program standards carefully
drawn to mandate program quality without being prescriptive in
terms of program design. The regulations governing Head Start
now provide detailed guidelines about program objectives,
performance standards, and operation (45 CFR 1303–1304).

Grantees and delegate agencies are required to develop
written plans covering the implementation of the program
according to detailed performance standards. The term "performance standards" refers to Head Start program function,
activities, and facilities required and necessary to meet the
objectives and goals of the Head Start program as they relate
directly to children and their families. Grantees must meet or
exceed these standards. While compliance with the performance
standards is required as a condition of federal funding, and
programs not in compliance may be terminated, it is expected
that the standards will be largely self-enforcing, drawing on
the official document describing Head Start performance standards (HHS, 1984B). The performance standards were published
in the Federal Register of June 30, 1975 (Volume 40, Number 126,
Part II).

Where Does Head Start Funding Come From?

Sharon Stephan (1986) of the Congressional Research Service describes Project Head Start as a federal matching grant
program with funds allocated to states on the basis of a formula

that takes into account the states' child poverty population and other factors. The Secretary of the HHS distributes funds to eligible Head Start agencies within each state. With certain exceptions, federal funds are limited to 80 percent of total program costs; there is a 20 percent non-federal matching requirement. About 13 percent of Head Start appropriations are reserved for Indian and migrant programs, payments to the territories, training and technical assistance, and discretionary payments. Federal law prohibits Head Start programs from charging fees for participants, although parents who wish to pay may do so. In 1993, approximately 721,268 children were served in 1,370 Head Start programs at a cost of $3,720 per child.

Current Status of Project Head Start

Today, Project Head Start is broad in both scope and services. Here we briefly review the number of programs, budgets, enrollments, the ages of the children served, the economic status of the children served, racial composition, multicultural services, and services to handicapped children. The statistics presented in this section are taken from the annual "Project Head Start Statistical Fact Sheet" prepared by the Administration on Children, Youth, and Families (HHS, 1993).

Number of Programs

For fiscal year (FY) 1992, there were 1,370 Head Start programs. There were 31,254 Head Start classrooms. These classrooms were supported by 109,345 paid staff and 950,175 volunteers.

Budgets

The FY 1986 budget was $4,322,662,000. Of that amount, $2,120,862,000 was distributed among local Head Start projects. The remaining funds were allocated for training and technical assistance, monitoring/program review, and research, demonstration, and evaluation programs.

The estimated average cost to serve each Head Start child during 1992 was $3,415. For 1993, the projected average cost per child is $3,720. Table 1 indicates the 1992 Head Start budget for each state.

TABLE 1

Fiscal Year 1992 State Allocations for Head Start

State	Dollars	Enrollment
Alaska	4,434,437	1,067
Arizona	20,728,637	6,179
Arkansas	22,296,763	8,213
California	219,422,605	52,658
Colorado	19,353,453	6,604
Connecticut	18,694,186	5,311
Delaware	4,454,359	1,333
District of Columbia	9,672,836	2,639
Florida	67,551,798	20,567
Georgia	52,224,673	16,080
Hawaii	7,546,861	1,974
Idaho	6,745,366	1,658
Illinois	99,851,613	28,802
Indiana	31,054,289	10,213
Iowa	16,484,282	5,266
Kansas	14,175,344	4,705
Kentucky	38,053,223	12,467
Louisiana	48,205,498	15,804
Maine	9,476,491	3,132
Maryland	27,042,600	7,594
Massachusetts	42,347,763	10,159
Michigan	82,320,773	26,174
Minnesota	24,372,946	7,136
Mississippi	71,861,334	22,343
Missouri	35,641,002	11,972
Montana	6,436,066	1,961
Nebraska	10,284,375	3,154
Nevada	4,000,263	1,073

State	Dollars	Enrollment
New Hampshire	4,080,063	1,016
New Jersey	54,531,708	11,688
New Mexico	13,655,100	4,958
New York	153,857,920	34,688
North Carolina	44,259,298	14,083
North Dakota	4,283,464	1,458
Ohio	84,964,311	29,132
Oklahoma	24,077,616	8,977
Oregon	17,759,806	3,885
Pennsylvania	82,449,211	22,414
Puerto Rico	95,628,988	29,031
Rhode Island	6,964,242	2,293
South Carolina	27,716,497	9,025
South Dakota	5,421,037	1,691
Tennessee	39,270,696	12,481
Texas	113,611,730	36,394
Utah	10,668,599	3,403
Vermont	4,556,353	1,129
Virginia	33,134,302	9,455
Washington	27,533,158	6,361
West Virginia	18,959,237	5,842
Wisconsin	31,052,342	9,665
Wyoming	3,370,992	1,128
Outer Pacific	6,252,538	5,439
Virgin Islands	4,293,601	1,422
American Indian	65,914,802	17,559
Migrant Programs	87,839,902	27,211
Total	$2,120,862,000	621,078

Source: HHS, Project Head Start Statistical Fact Sheet, Washington, D.C., 1993.

Overall Enrollments

The total enrollment for Head Start in fiscal year (FY) 1992 was 621,078. As indicated in Table 2, Head Start enrollment between 1965 and 1969 was more than 500,000 children. Enrollment levels dropped below 400,000 children between 1970 and 1982.

TABLE 2

Enrollments and Congressional Appropriations for Project Head Start, 1965 to 1993

Fiscal Year	Enrollment	Appropriation
1965	561,000	$96,400,000
1966	733,000	198,900,000
1967	681,400	349,200,000
1968	693,900	316,200,000
1969	663,600	333,900,000
1970	477,400	325,700,000
1971	397,500	360,000,000
1972	379,000	376,300,000
1973	379,000	400,700,000
1974	352,800	403,900,000
1975	349,000	403,900,000
1976	349,000	441,000,000
1977	333,000	475,000,000
1978	391,400	625,000,000
1979	387,500	680,000,000
1980	376,300	735,000,000
1981	387,300	818,700,000
1982	395,800	911,700,000
1983	414,950	912,000,000
1984	442,140	995,750,000
1985	452,080	1,075,059,000
1986	451,732	1,040,315,000*
1987	451,732	1,130,542,000
1988	448,464	1,206,324,000
1989	450,970	1,235,000,000
1990	540,930	1,552,000,000
1991	583,471	1,951,800,000
1992	621,078	2,201,800,000
1993	721,268**	2,776,289,600

*Post-Gramm-Rudman
**Projected enrollment for fiscal year 1993
Source: HHS, Project Head Start Statistical Fact Sheet, Washington, D.C., 1993.

Since 1982, enrollments have increased to levels above 400,000 children.

In 1965, the pilot year, Head Start was a summer program only. From 1966 to 1981, children were enrolled both full and part time. Since 1982, only full-year services have been provided. Overall, a total of 12,040,000 children have been served by the program since it began in 1965.

Still, Head Start serves only a fraction of the eligible children. According to the U.S. Bureau of the Census (1988), there were 5 million Head Start eligible children, five years old and younger, living in the United States. Head Start served one out of five eligible three- to five-year-old children, and only 13,000 of the possible 2.5 million children under age three. Although kindergarten programs were available to the large majority of Head Start eligible five-year-old children, and an unknown number of Head Start eligible three- and four-year-olds were served in state funded preschools, the demand for Head Start services continues to be tremendous (NHSA, 1990).

Ages of Children Served

For FY 1987 and 1992, the ages of the children served are reported in Table 3.

TABLE 3
Ages of Head Start Children

	1987	1992
five-year-olds and older	13 percent	7 percent
four-year-olds	59 percent	61 percent
three-year-olds	26 percent	27 percent
under three years of age	2 percent	3 percent

Source: HHS, Project Head Start Statistical Fact Sheet, Washington, D.C., 1993.

Economic Status of Children Served

By definition, Head Start serves children and families who have limited financial resources. For example, in 1992, 68 percent of Head Start families had incomes of less than $9,000 per year, and 84 percent had yearly incomes of less than $12,000 (HHS Project Head Start Statistical Fact Sheet, 1993).

While Head Start primarily serves children with incomes below the poverty line, some non-poor children are also served. The original Head Start planning committee agreed that economic segregation was not desirable and that Head Start should provide opportunities for children from different income groups to learn from each other (Richmond, Stipek, and Zigler, 1979). Since 1965, Head Start has provided that up to 10 percent of the children served could be drawn from above the poverty line. However, because of funding limitations, many local programs have found it difficult to meet the needs of the poor and at the same time promote economic integration. The lowest income families are given preference (NHSA, 1990, p. 30).

Further, the most needy children appear to benefit most from Project Head Start (the most needy are defined as children from families whose mother had a tenth grade education or less, children of single-parent families, and children with low cognitive scores when they entered Head Start). An exception to this pattern is that children from small families gained more than children from large families (Collins and Deloria, 1983).

The National Head Start Association Silver Ribbon Panel (NHSA, 1990) indicated concern over the lack of flexibility of Head Start income guidelines. The panel argued that:

- Head Start eligibility requirements are more stringent than for other federal programs.

- Local cost of living or family circumstances may require flexibility to allow participation of more than 10 percent of "at-risk families" who are above federal poverty guidelines. This is particularly relevant where no other services, or limited services, are available.

• If Head Start is to encourage continuity of services and economic self-sufficiency, there may be a need for flexibility of the income guidelines or a sliding fee scale.

Racial Composition

Since about 90 percent of Head Start families are below the poverty line, it is not surprising that Head Start serves a large number of children of color. These children comprise at least two-thirds of Head Start's enrollment. Table 4 indicates the racial composition of children served in 1986 and 1992.

TABLE 4
Racial Composition of Head Start Children

	1986	*1992*
American Indian	4 percent	4 percent
Hispanic	21 percent	23 percent
Black	40 percent	37 percent
White	32 percent	33 percent
Asian	3 percent	3 percent

Source: HHS Project Head Start Statistical Fact Sheet, Washington, D.C., 1993

There appear to be small decreases in the proportion of black children and small increases in the proportion of Hispanic and white children.

Royster and his colleagues (1978) observed that the participation of minorities, especially blacks and Hispanics, is twice as high as their proportion in the poverty population, while the percentage of white children is approximately one-half of their proportion in the poverty population. These participation rates illustrate that Head Start has served the children and families of the ethnic and racial groups that are overrepresented among the poor (Laosa, 1985).

Research indicates that children of color generally demonstrate impressive gains in Head Start, although according to Collins and Deloria (1983), this was not equally true in all Head Start program settings. Intermediate cognitive gains were greater for Head Start children "in classes with less than half or more than 90 percent minority enrollment" (CSR, 1985). However, critics note that the "less than half" claim is based on only two experimental studies (Schweinhart and Weikart, 1986).

Multicultural Services

Appropriately, Head Start offers a number of multicultural services. For example, the children of migrant workers have been of special concern to Head Start (Valentine, 1979). Since 1969, Head Start has offered programs for migrant children, with the most important aspect of these programs being flexibility of programming. Migrant Head Start programs operate for very long hours, sometimes from 4:00 A.M. to midnight, with open enrollment to infants and toddlers as well as four- and five-year-olds. Valentine further states that Head Start programs for migrants have reached only 2 percent of these young children. Health, education, and nutrition specialists follow children as their parents follow the crops. However, previous research indicated that migrant children experienced greater difficulties than other Head Start children in being immunized and gaining access to other health services such as dental care (Collins and Deloria, 1983).

Given that Hispanic children now comprise about 23 percent of all Head Start children, special efforts are made to meet their special developmental and cultural needs. Projects have been funded to develop curricula providing instruction in two languages for Spanish-speaking children and to establish resource centers providing technical assistance to Head Start grantees with programs for Spanish-speaking children and families (Richmond, Stipek, and Zigler, 1979).

Indeed, linguistic diversity is a significant issue in many Head Start programs, as indicated in Tables 5 and 6. Only 37 percent of all local Head Start programs are English monolingual, while a full 63 percent of the programs have children who use two or more languages. Indeed, many programs have children who use three, four, five, and six or more languages—a work-a-day reality that boggles the imagination (Ellsworth Associates, 1993).

TABLE 5

Dominant Language of Head Start Children, 1990–1991

English	413,146
Spanish	81,541
Vietnamese	2,319
Chinese	1,682
Hmong	1,576
Haitian	1,542
Cambodian	1,275
French	326
Korean	315
Japanese	33
Other	12,266

Source: Ellsworth Associates, 1993.

Since its inception, Head Start has been a leader in requiring that the home, cultural, and ethnic background of children and their families be an integral component of the program. Slaughter et al. (1988) remind us that Head Start performance standards specify that "the education services component shall provide for a supportive social and emotional climate which provides an environment of acceptance which helps each child build ethnic pride, develop a positive self-concept. . . ." Curricular and teaching strategies recommended in the performance standards include showing respect for each child, respecting and protecting individual rights and belongings, acknowledging and accepting the unique qualities of each child, avoiding situations that stereotype sex roles and racial/ethnic backgrounds, accepting each child's language, and fostering the child's comfort in using the primary language. "Head Start's interpretation of what a multicultural program entails is broad and focuses on the child's lifestyle and pattern of social interaction at many levels, including the family and the community as well as ethnic and cultural background" (Slaughter et al., 1988, p. 6). Head Start has developed several bilingual and multicultural curricula for use in conjunction with the national curriculum in order to provide programs that meet the needs of children within the context of their ethnic and cultural backgrounds (Arenas, 1980; Slaughter et al., 1988).

Along with an official memorandum (dated March 5, 1991) to all Head Start grantees and delegate agencies, former ACYF Commissioner Wade F. Horn sent to grantees a landmark document, "Multicultural Principles for Head Start Programs," for "their consideration and use." The principles detailed in this important document are the result of two years of effort by the Head Start Multicultural Task Force, a group convened by ACYF to consider the current needs of grantees who are serving very diverse populations in many parts of the country. In this memorandum, Horn further stated that "these principles now stand as a challenge to Head Start grantees and delegate agencies to focus efforts on individualizing services so that every child and family feels respected and valued and is able to grow in accepting and appreciating differences. [These principles] form the foundation of our joint efforts to help both the families we serve and the staff we employ to make every effort to understand and respect our differences." Horn further exhorted each Head Start director to give wide attention to these principles "since the issue of multicultural programming impinges on all of the Head Start components and services."

The ability of Head Start to meet the difficult challenges posed by the increasing ethnic and language diversity of the population it seeks to serve will continue to be the topic of much scrutiny. As the Head Start population becomes increasingly diverse, it becomes clear that there is a scarcity of adequate and pertinent data to inform policy and practice.

Also clear is, as Ellsworth Associates (1993) point out,

> Head Start families and children are not all alike. The problems faced by an African-American child growing up in an inner city neighborhood are only broadly like those of a Native American child on an Indian reservation, a child growing up in a depressed area of Appalachia, or a Spanish-speaking child in the migrant stream. It is essential that future research and evaluation on the efficacy of Head Start address the program effects for these diverse populations.

TABLE 6
Number of Monolingual and Multilingual Head Start Programs in 1988

English only	672
Spanish only	38
Chinese only	1
Other	8
Total, one dominant language	719
Two dominant languages	536
Three dominant languages	254
Four dominant languages	134
Five dominant languages	84
Six dominant languages	63
Seven dominant languages	20
Eight dominant languages	11
Nine dominant languages	12
Ten dominant languages	2
Total, more than one dominant language	1,116
Total programs	1,835

Source: Ellsworth Associates, 1993.

Children with Disabilities

Head Start has a strong record of including a sizeable number of preschool handicapped children on a systematic basis (see HEW, 1980). In 1972, Congress mandated that at least 10 percent of Head Start's national enrollment consist of handicapped children (on a statewide basis as of 1974).

Valentine (1979) lists two objectives of the legislative mandate: to provide necessary services for individual handicapped children in a mainstreamed environment, and to coordinate services with other agencies servicing handicapped children. In Head Start, an interdisciplinary diagnostic team designs an individualized program plan for each child. Most programs provide preservice and inservice training for staff working with handicapped children, but reported that further training was still needed.

Table 7 presents the frequency of disabilities among enrolled Head Start children. As can be seen, speech impairments were by far the most common form of diagnosed disability among this population (71 percent), which is not surprising, given the age of Head Start enrollees. Children with low-incidence, high-severity handicaps such as sensory impairments or autism are likely to be identified earlier than children with high incidence handicaps such as learning or emotional disturbance, which are less severe and typically identified after the preschool period (Hall, 1992). Future research is needed to detect these more common developmental impairments, which may respond to early intervention.

Handicapped children accounted for 61,898 children or 12.2 percent of all children enrolled in full-year Head Start programs in FY 1985. By 1992, 13.4 percent of the Head Start enrollment were children with disabilities (mental retardation, health impairments, visual handicaps, hearing impairments, emotional disturbances, speech and language impairments, orthopedic handicaps, and learning disabilities). Previous research indicated that although Head Start is serving a number of severely and profoundly handicapped children, the majority are classified as mildly to moderately handicapped (Collins and Deloria, 1983).

Head Start has been shown to improve the cognitive skills of children with certain kinds of handicaps (Collins and Deloria, 1983). Children diagnosed as speech impaired outperformed their peers who were not in Head Start or other preschool programs. Children with learning disabilities or emotional disturbances also performed better on some measures of intellectual achievement. Head Start did not appear to have a measurable effect on the cognitive development of mentally retarded or physically handicapped children. Overall, however, Head Start services to the handicapped compared favorably to those of non-Head Start programs, even though the latter tended to have larger per pupil expenditures.

TABLE 7

Frequency and Percent of Disabilities among Enrolled Head Start Children in 1991 and 1992

Primary Disability	Frequency	Percent of Diagnosed Disabilities
Blindness	111	0.1
Visual Impairment	1,097	1.4
Deafness	119	0.1
Hearing Impairment	1,136	1.5
Physical Impairment	2,657	3.4
Speech Impairment	54,794	70.9
Health Impairment	7,251	9.4
Mental Impairment	2,512	3.3
Emotional Impairment	3,323	4.3
Learning Disability	4,267	5.5

Source: Ellsworth Associates, 1993.

Summary

This brief "primer" demonstrates the scope and breadth of services offered and people reached through Project Head Start. Project Head Start is extraordinarily diverse. Its primary strength is its capacity to be flexible and to respond sensitively to changing social and public policy conditions. As we will see later, rapid change and expansion have challenged Head Start's administrative capacity, perceptions of its effectiveness, and its ability to deliver consistently high quality services in every location.

PART B

*Models and Strategies
for the Twenty-First Century*

CHAPTER 4

Overview of Models and Strategies for the Twenty-First Century

Introduction

Head Start, as the largest early childhood program in the United States, has played a key leadership role in service delivery and research that has impacted the entire child development field. This leadership role has served many purposes: It has strengthened support for early childhood in both the public and private sectors; fostered understanding of the developmental needs of children in the early elementary years; promoted linkages between the early childhood community and other educational or social services; and demonstrated successful "models that work" for poor children and families.

Program Options

In the early years, Head Start achieved its instant and continuing popularity by focusing essentially on one "model" of service: organized preschool centers. This exclusive focus was adopted as a matter of administrative policy, not of statute. Indeed, Head Start centers were so popular in both public and congressional circles that it became difficult either by statutory authorization or administrative action to implement alternative models. A traditional classroom-based program in which educational activities were enriched by other services was vigorously promulgated. Alternative forms of delivering services to

children, such as in-home services, parent education, and prenatal care, were viewed as attempts to undercut the "model"
(Harmon and Hanley, 1979).

Yet by the period 1968–1972, Head Start's innovative
character was weakening and had evolved into a fairly rigid
delivery system committed to a single, classroom-based design—
whether or not that design was the most appropriate for a
particular child or community. Partly as a response to criticisms
of the project resulting from the Westinghouse report, program
options were initiated as part of Head Start's "improvement and
innovation" efforts (Harmon and Hanley, 1979).

Beginning in April 1973, Head Start programs were
permitted to consider several program models in addition to the
standard Head Start model. Grantees were encouraged to select
the program option best suited to the needs of the children
served and the capabilities and resources of the program staff.
Head Start grantees could support any option or design, provided that the community could demonstrate that it would result
in a quality child development program at reasonable cost and
meet Head Start guidelines.

Five program options were identified: the standard Head
Start model, variations in center attendance, double sessions,
home-based models, and locally designed variations.

The standard Head Start model was defined as a
continuation of the five-day week, center-based classroom
format. In 1973, grantees were advised to carefully assess their
needs and capabilities to determine whether another program
option might be more effective.

In variations of the center attendance option, Head Start
programs could elect to serve some or all children on a less than
five day per week basis. All children who attended Head Start
on a partial basis had to receive the same comprehensive
developmental services as full-day children. Shortened hours in
the classroom could be supplemented by a parent education
program or another option that would assist parents in
developing their role as educators of their own children.
Examples of variations in attendance plans are split session
schedules (two regularly enrolled groups each meeting two days
per week with the fifth day set aside for activities such as

inservice training or home visits) or the four day per week schedule with the fifth day used for special activities.

The double sessions option, it was cautioned, could not be required or permitted solely as a cost-saving device. In this option, different children were scheduled to attend morning or afternoon sessions. Provisions had to be made to ensure high quality instruction, food, and individualization in both sessions.

Today, the average Head Start program provides services thirty-four weeks per year. Most Head Start programs (82 percent) are half day, 10 percent are full day, and 8 percent are a combination of full and half day (Stephan, 1986).

Home-based models focus on the parent as the primary factor in the child's development and the home as the central facility. These programs must meet several conditions including the provision of comprehensive services, a curriculum and the requisite materials for each child, a parent program, weekend and evening services when needed, career development opportunities for staff, a service delivery system, a staff selection program in accord with staff responsibilities, staff development, and opportunities for using volunteers.

In addition to the above four models, local programs can elect to design and propose options that they felt were appropriate for their children and communities. These locally designed options must be derived from an analysis of the standard model, be consistent with good child development practice, be comprehensive, and be consistent with all performance standards.

Head Start Improvements and Innovations

Harmon and Hanley (1979) explain that program options were part of an overall Head Start improvement and innovation effort. Other innovations which were devised at that time were:

1. The performance standards.
2. Mandated self-assessment by local grantees as an integral part of the Head Start refunding cycle. This was an attempt to encourage an impetus for improvement and innovation at the local level.

3. The creation of a program development and innovation staff at the national level. A primary focus was the integration of program components.

4. The conversion from summer to full-year programs.

5. Development and dissemination of program options.

6. The launching of the Child Development Associate (CDA) staff training program.

7. An enhanced emphasis on parent involvement (Harmon and Hanley, 1979; Collins and Deloria, 1983).

An Array of Models and Strategies

In addition to program options, the new program development and innovation initiatives created a series of national demonstrations to test and promulgate alternative designs. Descriptions of some of these special projects are as follows:

- *Parent and Child Centers* were initially launched in 1967 as a preventive program providing comprehensive services to low-income families with children up to three years of age. There are 106 centers currently in operation around the country. The primary objectives of the program are the improvement of the overall developmental progress of the child, with emphasis on the prevention of a variety of developmental deficits, increasing parents' knowledge of their own children, enhancing parental skills, and strengthening the family unit.

- *Home Start*, for children age three to five, was founded in 1972 to provide Head Start services to children and families in their homes. Home-based services allow isolated families, particularly in rural areas, to receive Head Start's educational, health, and social services. In 1989, more than 500 Head Start programs included some home-based services (NHSA, 1990).

- Thousands of parents have found work, job skills, and career development through Head Start development opportunities.

- *Child and Family Resource Programs* were pioneered by Head Start in the 1980s and targeted to children and families from the prenatal period through age eight. These programs were designed to provide a variety of services from which families could choose according to their needs. A family advocate worked with each family to provide or make available prenatal care, developmental programs, pediatric care, programs to facilitate a smooth transition from preschool to elementary school, and general support services.

- *Project Developmental Continuity* began in 1974 to offer Head Start-related services to children throughout the first three years of primary school. Special emphasis was placed on maintaining parent involvement and on the needs of handicapped and bilingual children.

- *Comprehensive Child Development Programs*, five-year demonstration projects for pregnant women and mothers with children under age one, were funded by Congress in 1988 (Besharov, 1992).

- There are many local Head Start programs that now provide concrete instruction for parents in infant and child care, health care, and nutrition (Besharov, 1992). Washington's Wide Opportunities for Women program has a slogan: "Teach the Mother and Reach the Child."

- In 1991, the Head Start Bureau funded thirty-two *substance abuse* projects in local centers (Besharov, 1992).

- In 1991, the Head Start Bureau funded eleven *family support* projects for such problems as teenage pregnancy, homelessness, and family violence (Besharov, 1992).

- In Washington, D.C., Head Start staff members work informally with the local department of employment services to ensure that spaces are reserved in the department's Job Opportunity and Basic Skills (JOBS) training programs for Head Start parents. Children are eligible for extended day care only if their parents are working or in job training full time (Besharov, 1992).

- In 1991, thirty-two *Head Start transition* projects were funded to demonstrate effective strategies for supporting children and families as they make the transition from Head Start through kindergarten and the first three grades of public school. The projects include Head Start grantees and public school systems. These projects are testing whether providing continuous comprehensive services to Head Start children will maintain and enhance the early benefits attained by the children and their families.

- *Health Start*, which operated from 1971 to 1974, provided Head Start-like health services to children under the age of six who were not being screened through any other program.

- *Project Follow Through*, established in 1967 for school-age children, was designed to continue and build on the cognitive and social gains made by children in Head Start or similar preschool programs.

- *The Child Development Associate (CDA) National Credentialing Program* was created by Head Start in 1971 to enhance the quality of child care by defining, evaluating, and recognizing the competence of child care providers and home visitors. The first CDA credential was awarded in July 1975. Within ten years, nearly 17,000 individuals earned a CDA credential, affecting nearly 750,000 young children and allowing one-quarter million parents to participate in the assessment of the teachers of their preschool children. Since 1975 more than 50,000 child care providers have earned the CDA credential. Also, forty-nine states and the District of Columbia have incorporated the credential into their child care licensing regulations (Council for Early Childhood Professional Recognition, July 1993).

- *Education for Parenthood* teaches Head Start parents and high school students about early childhood and human development through direct field experience in Head Start centers.

- Head Start collaboration with the *Medicaid Early and Periodic Screening, Diagnosis, and Treatment Program* (1974 to 1976) sought to make health services available to Medicaid-eligible children.

- Head Start has offered bilingual/multicultural approaches which focus on the diverse cultures represented in Head Start and on the needs of children whose primary language is not English. In 1989, more than 14,900 children were served in Indian Head Start programs and more than 19,000 in migrant Head Start programs (NHSA, 1990).

- In 1992, Congress allowed grantees to offer the program's health services to younger siblings of Head Start enrollees. While not all programs have the capacity to do this, those that provide the service make an important contribution to the healthy development of children (CDF, 1992).

Although Head Start has been a leader in launching local innovations, there have been few systematic efforts to disseminate promising practices within Head Start and to the larger early childhood and human services field (NHSA, 1990). Also, despite marked improvement in performance in relation to minimum program standards, Harmon and Hanley (1979) conclude that neither local agencies nor regional staffs fully exploited the opportunity to innovate. Still, partly as a result of these improvements and innovations, Collins and Deloria (1983) assert that Head Start grew more effective over the years. Research indicates that the impact of Head Start on children's intellectual development was roughly twice as great after 1970 as in 1969. This corresponds to the period in which several important improvements were introduced into Head Start.

Head Start as a Leader

The decade of the 1990s has ushered in an array of Head Start innovations. New initiatives have been launched in such critical areas as family literacy, substance abuse, increasing the employability of parents and other family members, and other areas related to family self-sufficiency. For example, in 1992, Head Start's parent support activities were strengthened by an act of Congress which requires that local programs offer or refer parents to literacy training and parenting education classes (CDF, 1992). Also, ACYF is fostering collaboration across federal and state government agencies such as the JOBS program.

In this chapter, we have outlined a brief history of Head Start program options, innovations, and special projects. In the following chapters, we want to illustrate Head Start's leadership role in developing effective models and strategies that work for economically disadvantaged communities. As examples of leadership, in Chapter 5 we present models for working with parents, a strong legacy of Head Start. Two critical issues, and Head Start's response to them, are presented in Chapter 6 (substance abuse) and Chapter 7 (involving men).

Working with Parents
The Legacy of Head Start

As Project Head Start celebrates its twenty-ninth anniversary, it is clearly recognized as one of the most successful and enduring antipoverty programs in the United States. The widely heralded effectiveness of Head Start is particularly important because the program directs attention to parent involvement as a means to assure a stable foundation for the educational, economic, and social progress of the children served.

Challenges to Family Involvement

It continues to be true that little is known about the impact of parent involvement, a crucial aspect of Head Start. We are convinced that the effectiveness of Head Start programs today is hampered by the relatively limited attention to family development. Further, changes in family structures and functions since the founding of Head Start have altered the ability of many families to take advantage of traditional Head Start services. Six trends in family life are particularly evident:

1. The feminization of poverty;
2. The rise in teen parenting;
3. The surge in the number of mothers of preschool children in the work force;
4. The increasing challenge for low-income families to attain economic self-sufficiency;

5. Substance abuse; and

6. Family and community violence.

These trends are often interrelated: The female poor are frequently teen mothers who may abuse illegal drugs or be involved in community violence. These changes in families indicate an urgent need for complementary changes in the services Head Start provides.

These six conditions in American families create new demands on individuals and on the programs that serve them. Sadly, these dramatic changes are probably not short term and are unlikely to be reversed. New family structures and roles are not automatically accommodated in federal programs, but the implications of these changes for Head Start must be explored by all professionals who are concerned about our nation's children. It is imperative that we consider possible changes because of Head Start's recognition of the importance of the family, rather than the school, as the ultimate source of a child's values and behavior (Zigler and Anderson, 1979, p. 14).

Clearly, parent involvement is and has been the hallmark of Head Start services. Yet effective parent involvement and empowerment strategies are increasingly difficult to plan and carry out for several reasons:

- The rising number of multi-problem families enrolling in the program (HHS, 1989A).

- The erosion of comprehensive services and family support. Extended families and other traditional supports are no longer typically available. Yet challenges such as the severity of poverty and the diversity of families have intensified. A NHSA (1990) survey indicates that many Head Start programs are finding that they need to provide expanded family support in order to encourage parent involvement in the program and in the lives of their children. At the same time, more individualized approaches to parent involvement are needed in order to respond to different family situations.

- The lack of adequate staff. Ironically, as the needs of Head Start families have intensified, many programs have been forced to eliminate or combine positions in order to reduce or contain costs. As one Head Start director put it, "How can we expect quality services from an employee where a job title is Bus Driver/Social Service and Home Visitor" (NHSA, 1990, p. 22). Studies sponsored by the Administration for Children, Youth, and Families illustrate heavy caseloads and make recommendations for improvement. The National Head Start Association (1990) analysis of these reports indicates a lack of full time health, parent involvement, and social service coordinators in a number of programs. About 84 percent of the grantees noted increased demands on staff time for such activities as one-to-one counseling, assistance to parents, and extra home visits. About two-thirds of the respondents said that staff was adversely affected by the stress, burnout, and frustration caused by these demands (HHS, OIG, 1989A, 1989B).

Despite these challenges, every Head Start project is expected to meet certain performance standards with respect to parent involvement.

Parent Involvement Performance Standards

In the Head Start performance standards, local programs are required to place greater priority on parent-child interaction and on the parental role in child development and learning. The parent involvement objectives for Head Start grantees are as follows:

1. Provide a planned program of experience and activities which support and enhance the parental role as the principal influence in the child's education and development.
2. Provide a program that recognizes the parents as:
   A. Responsible guardians of their children's well-being.
   B. Prime educators of their children.

C. Contributors to the Head Start program in their communities.

3. Provide the following kinds of opportunities for parent participation:

A. Direct involvement in decision making in program planning and operations.

B. Participation in classroom and other program activities as paid employees, volunteers, or observers.

C. Activities for parents that they have helped to develop.

D. Working with their own children in cooperation with Head Start staff.

The parent involvement plan should address four areas: parent participation; the development of parenting skills; communication among program management, program staff, and parents; and communication among parents, area residents, and the program. These areas are specified as follows:

1. Assure the voluntary participation of parents in accordance with the *Head Start Policy Manual,* Instruction 1– 31, Section B2, The Parents (ACYF Transmittal Notice 70.2, August 10, 1970). This part of the policy manual also appears in the *Federal Register,* Volume 40, Number 126, June 30, 1975. The parent policy contains:

A. An introduction which highlights the belief that the gains made by the child in Head Start must be understood and built on by the family and the community.

B. An outline of at least four major kinds of parent participation (see item 3, above).

2. Provide methods and opportunities for involving parents in experiences and activities which enhance the development of their skills, their self-confidence, their sense of independence, their role as the primary influence in their children's lives, their roles as educators of their children, their ability to identify and use community resources, their opportunities for self-enrichment

and employment, and their understanding of health, mental health, dental, and nutritional needs.

3. Ensure effective two-way communication between staff and parents on a regular basis throughout the program year.

4. Establish effective procedures by which parents and area residents can influence the character of programs affecting their interests.

The History of Parent Involvement in Head Start

Parent participation has been a key element of Project Head Start since its inception. The Cooke memo of 1965 (Zigler and Valentine, 1979), which formed the philosophical basis of Head Start, emphasized the role of the family and the community. Recognizing that parents have a privileged role in child development, both the development and operation of Head Start programs have stressed parent participation and involvement. Parent involvement in the various aspects of the Head Start program is mandated by law.

Further, all of the program component areas (education, health, social services, and parent involvement) outlined in the 1972 Head Start performance standards address the role of Head Start parents. Indeed, over time, "recipient" participation, as required by Head Start guidelines, was interpreted to mean participation by the parent, rather than by representatives from the larger community (Harmon and Hanley, 1979).

Head Start can accurately be credited with launching the trend toward parent involvement in education and social services (Harmon and Hanley, 1979). The goal is to provide parents with the knowledge and services that would enable them to improve their economic status and to provide a favorable developmental environment for their children (Zigler, 1979). Indeed, the opportunities that allow Head Start parents to plan and operate programs contrast sharply with typical practices in public schools.

There is a wide range of parent activities in Head Start: advisory board memberships, classroom teachers, volunteers and aides, participants in parent meetings, and participation in structured parent programs (Slaughter, 1982). Also, every Head Start program has a policy council, at least 50 percent of whose members are Head Start parents. Through the policy councils, parents are involved in decisions about the operation of the centers, including personnel matters and the allocation of funds.

During the 1970s, Head Start began several initiatives to broaden parent involvement and to test innovative strategies for strengthening families. Home Start, the Child and Family Resource Program, and Project Developmental Continuity all began during this time frame. Yet during the rapid program expansions during the 1980s, "quality," as indicated by perceptions of support activities for parent involvement, began to decline. However, the following list indicates the range of initiatives disseminated during this period:

1976—Exploring parenting (parent education curriculum)

1978—A guide for involving parents in Head Start

1982—Exploring self-sufficiency series

1985—Parent involvement component videotape

1985—Adult literacy demonstrations

1985—Family needs assessment model instrument

1985—Looking at life series (parent education curriculum)

1986—Parent enrichment curriculum (see R. Johnson, 1986)

The actual extent of parent participation in Head Start has not been fully documented. Estimates of the extent of parent volunteers in Head Start vary from three parents for every four children enrolled to ten parents per fifteen children (CDF, 1984). Nevertheless, a smaller core of parents probably provides the majority of volunteer hours. Limitations to parent involvement have been identified as transportation, child care, parliamentary procedure, and frequent rotation of parents (Payne et al., 1973). Critics also charge that, while the principle of parent involvement is widely accepted, its implementation varies greatly (Payne et al., 1973; Caliguri, 1970).

Research to date has also failed to identify the most productive kinds of parent involvement activities. Robinson and Choper (1979) have further charged that national evaluations have generally failed to assess the contributions of parents to Head Start programs or the benefits parents have received from their participation.

Suggesting that parents benefit psychologically and socially from their participation, Emmerich, et al. (cited in Lapides and Lapides, 1981) reported that parents participating in Head Start and nonparticipating parents differed in several characteristics. Their findings revealed that participating parents were more sensitive to their children's social, emotional, and intellectual needs; more affectionate and less likely to use punishment; more likely to use complex language with their children; more likely to reason with their children; more apt to pursue their own educational development; and more likely to use community agencies.

Research has clearly indicated, however, that parents approve of Head Start. Head Start has had a demonstrably positive impact on parent attitudes toward, and interactions with, their children. Further, parent involvement enhances the effectiveness of the program: the children of parents who have high levels of participation performed better on tests of achievement and development (Grotberg, 1969). Head Start parents also tend to remain involved in their children's education once the children enter elementary school (Midco, 1972), thereby illustrating that these parents want to be involved in the education of their children and that their children benefit when they do (Richmond, Stipek, and Zigler, 1979).

Head Start: Career Development or Child Development?

An assessment of the effects of Head Start on children cannot avoid the issue of the effect of the program on staff and parents because of the direct and immediate impact which staff and parents may have on the educative functions of the program.

As in most day care settings, special training in child development or early childhood education is generally not a prerequisite to employment in Head Start. An important aspect of staffing in Head Start programs has been the use of those persons most familiar with the children and their backgrounds: parents. Head Start has provided jobs to hundreds of thousands of parents and community residents. About 35 percent of paid staff are current or former Head Start parents, a consistent percentage since at least 1988 (Brush, Gaidurgis, and Best, 1993).

Omwake (1979) has suggested that with the emphasis on the use of parents and neighborhood residents as paraprofessionals, which emerged in 1967, the employment function of Head Start took precedence over the educative functions, with deleterious consequences for the quality of the latter.

The assumption guiding the use of parents and neighborhood residents as teaching staff is that local residents have a better understanding of the needs and nature of neighborhood children and their parents than do professionals. Thus, professional training is considered only one indicator of competence, with the consequence that Head Start staffs are composed of individuals with a wide variety of professional and personal competencies. The differences vary from program to program. Omwake argues that while it may be desirable to have varied competencies among staff, it is undesirable to permit variations in personal qualifications for working with the children. She regards it as particularly unfortunate and a serious defect that there are no definitive guidelines about qualifications for Head Start staff.

Omwake believes that Head Start's career development program for adults has achieved the immediate objective of providing encouragement and opportunities for staff members to improve their skills and become suitable teachers for Head Start children. However, she maintains that improvements in staff education have not resulted in a consistently improved educational experience for children in all Head Start programs.

Current Issues in Parent Involvement

There are several additional issues of current concern with respect to parent involvement. These issues include needs (1) to revitalize parent participation; (2) to view Head Start conceptually as a two-generation strategy; (3) to assess differences in the intensity of parent involvement; (4) to examine the role of the program on economic self-sufficiency; (5) to explore parent involvement as a means of personal growth; and (6) to review indices of quality in the parent involvement component.

Revitalizing Parent Participation

Parent involvement activities can be an appropriate and effective means of advancing the skills and knowledge of Head Start parents. These skills and knowledge may extend far beyond child development information. Rather, the process skills which Head Start parents may acquire through their involvement in Head Start—practice in negotiating with public institutions, enhanced leadership experiences, exercising control over aspects of their lives—may be, over the long term, even more important in disrupting the cycle of poverty.

Thus the concept of parent participation in programs such as Head Start is of critical importance. As parent skills and knowledge are enhanced, children benefit. Networks of these parents and children may be better prepared to cope with a less-supportive public school environment. Parents may be more aware of, and better able to address, discontinuities between their home cultures and the expectations of the schools. Indeed, the parents can be transformed into agents of social change (Knitzer, 1972).

While the concept of parent involvement is appropriate, the actual implementation of the idea may need to be revitalized. Some grantees have a paternalistic attitude toward parents which prevents parents from playing a decisive role in these projects (Richmond, Stipek, and Zigler, 1979). There is also concern that new Head Start innovations, related to new or existing grants, do not recognize the value of parent opinion as an empowerment tool.

Serving Two Generations

In order to counteract the intergenerational transmission of poverty, Head Start must focus on both the child and the parent. "In the old days we use to say, 'Give us children for a few hours a day and we will save them,'" says Wade Horn, former commissioner of ACYF and the senior federal administrator for the Head Start program (quoted in Besharov, 1992A, 1992B). "Now we know that we have to work within the entire family context, that if we are going to save children, we have to save the family, and that means working with the parents."

Thus 1989 studies by the U.S. Department of Health and Human Services reported that 84 percent of all Head Start programs used staff time and other resources to address family problems unrelated to child care. This approach, called "two-generation programming," attempts to reach children earlier with more intense developmental services, help low-income parents nurture and teach their own children, and encourage unemployed parents to work or continue their education (Besharov, 1992A, 1992B). Up to now, individual Head Start programs have used their own funds, and the Head Start Bureau has used time-limited research projects, to provide two-generational services, at least on a small scale. Sheila Smith (1991) points out that, in the absence of a program strategy for family support, it is difficult to set boundaries and expectations for local Head Start programs. Further, research and evaluation efforts are limited if each program initiative is examined independently (also see Smith, Blank, and Bond, 1990).

The Intensity of Parent Involvement

Any discussion of parent involvement must quickly acknowledge the fact that evaluations of the impact of the parent involvement component of Head Start are rather limited and largely anecdotal. Valentine and Stark (1979) suggest that the effects of parent involvement have been as varied as the character of the parent involvement component of the program. There are many case studies that offer examples of how parent involvement successfully mobilizes parents. There are other examples where parent involvement, either because of a lack of participation or the ineffectiveness of this component of the program, resulted in very little change in families. In assessing the impact of Head Start families, it is clear that there exists a wide variation in the extent, type, and intensity of their involvement in the program. These factors would, of course, affect the benefits from this component of the program.

As a result of this variation, many studies have focused on a comparison of the highly involved families with those who are less involved. Midco (1972B) found that Head Start parents who were highly involved in the learner role and decision-making role appeared most satisfied, showed more self-confidence and higher self-esteem, had a greater sense of internal focus of control and greater assurance about their future, were more involved in more efforts to change community institutions, and were more prevalent in high quality programs. In other words, high involvement improved parent and child attitudes and behavior, and it also improved program quality. Further, high involvement influenced positive changes in community institutions such as the social service and health programs. A major criticism of the study is that these differences could have existed between the highly involved and the less involved prior to the Head Start experience.

Parent Involvement and Economic Self-sufficiency

In the current atmosphere of "welfare reform" initiatives focused on the employment of public assistance recipients, a key question involves the impact of Head Start on economic self-sufficiency. In another national study of the long-term effects of Head Start, Collins (1983) reports that 7 percent of parents indicated that Head Start had helped them to find a job and 9 percent indicated that Head Start had helped them to further their education. However, given the low percentage of those obtaining jobs, it is likely that these jobs were within Head Start.

In fact, we still know very little about the relationship of parent involvement to family members' ability to obtain and maintain jobs, the impact of parent involvement on the career ladder movement of Head Start families, the impact of Head Start on family income pattern, or the impact of Head Start on family members other than Head Start children.

In an effort to address the paucity of research in this area, Oyemade, Washington, and Gullo (1989) sought to provide empirical information on the relationship of parent involvement to the economic and social self-sufficiency of Head Start families and children. Specific questions addressed by the research were:

- What is the relationship between the Head Start experience and the economic and social self-sufficiency of Head Start families?

- What is the relationship between the level of Head Start center parent involvement activities and the economic and social self-sufficiency of Head Start families?

- What is the relationship between the intensity of parental involvement and the economic and social self-sufficiency of Head Start families?

The five major findings were:

1. Overall, the Head Start parents in this study were significantly better off at the time of the study than they were at the beginning of their Head Start experience. The number of families receiving public assistance had been reduced from 49.2 percent to 33.1 percent. A significant number of parents reported improvements in their economic status. For example, only 20.4 percent of the families were above poverty level at the beginning of Head Start involvement; 27.8 percent were above the poverty level at the time of the study. Similarly, 37.9 percent of mothers were working as compared to 23.2 percent when their children began Head Start. Among the fathers, 74.2 percent were employed versus 68.4 percent before their Head Start experience. Home ownership also increased from 20.8 percent to 25.7 percent. College credit or degrees were earned by 38.5

percent of the mothers, compared to only 27.7 percent before Head Start involvement. Also, 31.1 percent of the fathers earned college credit or degrees compared to only 23.4 percent before Head Start involvement.

2. To assess the impact of the Head Start parental involvement component on the upward mobility of parents, subjects from low- and high-involvement centers were compared at the beginning of their Head Start experience and a few years later. There were no significant differences between low- and high-involvement centers at the beginning of their Head Start experience. However, after their involvement in the program, the groups did differ significantly on family income, employment of the mother, and employment of the father.

   Significantly more of the high-involvement parents (34 percent compared to 19 percent) were above the poverty level. Similarly, 60.4 percent of the parents from high-involvement centers were working full or part time, compared to only 35 percent of the parents from low-involvement centers. Also, 86.1 percent of the fathers from high-involvement centers were employed compared to only 55.1 percent from low-involvement centers.

3. Results indicated a significant positive relationship between intensity of Head Start parental involvement and preferred daily activities, family income, occupation, and education of the mother. Parents with higher social status responses, both at the beginning of their Head Start involvement and when the interview was administered, tended to have a generally greater intensity of involvement in Head Start activities. Similarly, parents with "higher education of mother" and "home ownership" had a greater intensity of involvement in career and job-related skill development activities.

4. The results of the study suggested that Head Start, and particularly its parental involvement component, has had a positive effect on the upward mobility of Head

Start parents. A significant number of parents whose children attended high-involvement Head Start centers are economically better off now than they were when their children began Head Start.

5. However, with regard to intensity of involvement, it appears that parents who are more involved in Head Start tend to be the relatively better-off parents from the beginning. Even though their economic status still improves through Head Start, it appears that the parents who take advantage of and benefit most from involvement opportunities are the relatively better-off parents. Still, we must bear in mind that the "better-off" parents are still in families with very low incomes.

Overall, these findings clearly suggest that Head Start parental involvement is an appropriate and effective way to advance the skills and knowledge of Head Start parents far beyond the acquisition of child development information. Because Head Start has been successful in helping families move up the socioeconomic ladder, expanded efforts in the area of parental involvement might result in even more significant gains. For example, while a significant number of Head Start families moved out of poverty, more than 70 percent remained in poverty.

Parent Involvement as a Means of Personal Growth

In another study, "Who Gets Involved? Head Start Mothers as Persons," Slaughter, Lindsay, Nakagawa, and Kuehne (1989) investigated parents' opinions of typical parental involvement activities. Specifically, they sought to determine which activities were reported effective for personal growth. Also of interest was determining whether parents chose activities based on the type of center program in which they participated.

Additionally, the personality of the parent was investigated as an important component in the parent's level of participation. The literature on possible "internal effects" of Head Start parent program activities suggest that self-esteem and parental involvement would be related. However, prior to this exploratory study, there was no research data on this topic which involved Head Start parents. It was assumed that parents whose self-esteem and ego development were higher could be expected to choose activities that were different from those of parents who had less self-confidence and lower levels of ego development.

There were three major findings of this study:

1. There was evidence that the Head Start center may contribute significantly to the level of parental involvement by increasing the availability of options to parents interested in these activities. While these results indicate that parents were getting involved in many activities, the activities primarily focused on were those in which parents did not have the opportunity to make decisions or to work on an equal level with their children's teachers. Is the lack of high involvement in activities a function of the center environment or of the parents' unwillingness to participate? Perhaps parents need more opportunities to participate in decision-making activities and leadership positions.

2. There was a significant relationship between involvement at high levels and ego development. This relationship suggests that parents experienced personal development through participation in these program activities. These findings are further supported by the relationship discerned between self-esteem and parental involvement at medium levels and the trend toward significance obtained at high-involvement levels. Although the authors did not conclusively eliminate the possibility that parents involved with these activities had a higher level of ego development from the outset, it was suggested that many parents would personally benefit from the experience of working in Head Start programs at a decision-making level.

3. Also, the findings support the literature that assumes that parental involvement in Head Start benefits the parents' personal growth and development. This literature is important because it describes how entire

families untimately may be enriched through their child's participation in a quality educational program. Given that the staff of the Head Start child's care depends on the family, it is extremely important that the child's most probable advocates be strengthened and supported with available program resources.

In a similar study, Parker et al. (1987) assessed the impact of parental involvement on the psychological well-being (i.e., presence or absence of psychological symptoms, self-esteem, social integration and attitudes about others and the community, life satisfaction, and feelings of mastery) of Head Start mothers. Results indicated that mothers' gains in psychological well-being were related to their participation in the supportive activities offered by Head Start. In particular, the mothers' psychological symptoms decreased, feelings of mastery increased, and satisfaction with the current quality of life increased.

Indices of Quality in the Parent Involvement Component

In an effort to synthesize information related to Head Start quality, Brush, Gaidurgis, and Best (1993) examined many areas of Head Start practice, including the parent involvement component. Three primary Head Start data bases were used: The Program Information Report, the On-Site Program Review Instrument (OSPRI), and the Head Start Cost Management System.

The researchers found that:

1. All grantees designated at least one individual as the parent involvement coordinator. Annual salaries for high school graduates were $14,228; salaries for coordinators with graduate degrees averaged $23,838.

2. Many coordinators tend to work alone (42 percent) or supervise a small staff.

3. Parent involvement staff serve relatively large numbers of families; the mean case load is 228 families; 10 percent of grantees have case loads which exceed 500. (Note:

There is no recommended case load for parent involvement staff.)

4. The mean cost for parent involvement activities per child is $180. Grantees with higher costs per child for parent involvement had fewer OSPRI items out of compliance.

5. Grantees involve parents in various types of activities. A mean of 55 percent of parents are involved in parent education activities, and 85 percent of parents volunteer at least once per year (an increase since 1988 when the mean was 79 percent).

6. Grantees with lower enrollments are more successful at involving parents in educational activities and in volunteer work. The optimal level of funded enrollment was 650; grantees with enrollments above and below that number had more items out of compliance.

7. Grantees with more highly paid coordinators have higher parent participation in educational activities and volunteering. Further, grantees who paid higher salaries to coordinators had fewer OSPRI items out of compliance.

Clearly, most Head Start grantees deliver extensive services and meet almost all of the parent involvement performance standards. Indeed, 49 percent of all grantees met *all* performance standards for parent involvement. Yet grantees are consistently struggling in these areas and requesting more assistance (NHSA, 1990).

Conclusion

There is an urgent need for a systematic and thorough national evaluation of the parental involvement component of Project Head Start. Such an evaluation should include diverse but complementary measures of parental involvement and assess the parents' own perceptions. It should include direct observations of Head Start centers with differing patterns and rates of participation. Special attention should be paid to parental personality development in addition to long-term external effects.

Too often, lower socioeconomic parents, particularly parents of color, are described as if they were a homogeneous group. Personal preferences and choices rarely enter into discussions of how they organize and sustain their families or rear their children. As is true for parents generally, investigation of their values, beliefs, and attitudes rarely extends beyond the study of childrearing goals and attitudes. This is unfortunate because parents do not rear children in social vacuums. How they perceive and participate in surrounding social institutions inevitably influences their perspectives on their own families and children. We need more research into the self-perceptions of Head Start parents as adolescent and adult men and women who live and rear families in an extremely challenging and complex society. Given the current mandate for Head Start to be responsive to the changing needs of American families, what better way to begin than to discover Head Start parents as persons?

CHAPTER 6

Substance Abuse
Meeting Changing Social Conditions

One significant barrier to parent involvement can be family involvement in substance abuse. Drug abuse is one of the most serious and perplexing problems facing the Head Start community today. Not only do increased rates of addiction place the Head Start population at greater risk for high school dropout, unemployment, crime, incarceration, and continued poverty, but children prenatally exposed to substance abuse are now entering the Head Start system at an alarming rate.

Every community—regardless of location or income level—has been touched by drug abuse. Teenage drinking, drug dealing in elementary schools, and infants born with Fetal Alcohol Syndrome (FAS) and other drug-related problems are now common. Although currently school-age children seem to be using fewer drugs than in previous years, the United States still has the highest rate of illicit drug use of any industrialized nation (Johnston, O'Malley, and Bachman, 1988). This situation is foreboding for the Head Start-eligible populations, particularly low-income people or people of color:

- About 8 percent of women (4.8 million) between ages fifteen and forty-four used an illegal substance in the month prior to the 1990 National Household Survey on Drug Abuse (Collins and Anderson, 1991, p. 3).
- Use of illegal drugs increased in certain groups including young adults, African Americans, the unemployed, and residents of large metropolitan areas (Collins and Anderson, 1991).

• Perhaps the most dire vision of the future concerns the intravenous users of heroin, a drug that has remained predominantly the preserve of those with low incomes who live in the inner city. These people are now at high risk for exposure to the AIDS virus because they share needles.

Why should Head Start be concerned about drug abuse prevention? Aside from the compelling ethical responsibility to advocate on behalf of all children and families, Head Start also practices two of the most effective techniques for preventing drug abuse—teaching in appropriate programs and working with parents. Head Start work with young children and their parents can make a difference that we can see during the early child-rearing years, but we also know that the teaching and discipline affects children all their lives. In addressing the issue of substance abuse in the Head Start community, there is a need to focus on three areas:

• Primary prevention of substance abuse for Head Start children who are at risk for later drug use,
• Intervention for families at high risk for involvement in alcohol or drug abuse, or who are already abusing substances, and
• Training for staff to work with families and children who have been prenatally exposed to drugs.

Before we look at the components of a model drug-abuse prevention program that can readily be incorporated into Head Start, child care, or any other early childhood program, we need to be familiar with the roots of drug abuse and, in contrast, the long-term, positive social consequences of good programs for young children.

The Roots of Drug Abuse

Childrearing practices and community and social forces all play a role in determining whether children will tend to become drug abusers. All parents have dreams for their children—

dreams of economic security, good health, good education, a nice home, and a safe neighborhood. Some families have more barriers to overcome to achieve these dreams than others. Some have to fight poverty, crowded housing, inadequate health care, crime, illiteracy, unemployment, and/or ethnic stereotypes as they struggle to achieve their dreams of self-sufficiency. For other families, although finances are less of a concern, parents or children may be dealing with personality problems or difficulties in their personal or social lives.

As educators, we are aware that strong families have a much better chance of realizing their dreams for themselves and their children. Good teachers have always known how important the total childrearing environment—home and school and other important groups—is for children's future success. New research has shed more light on the decades of continuing work that demonstrates that childrearing styles have a tremendous effect on how people act and think throughout their lives.

Parent's attitudes and examples can greatly affect their childrens' behaviors. There is substantial evidence that the family has more influence on children's behavior than their friends do, even in adolescence (Larsen, 1972, 1974).

Because the family plays such a powerful role, we need to be aware of how family factors can influence children's development and how well-designed programs can help families choose childrearing styles that will increase their children's chance to lead successful, productive lives.

There are several feelings common among people who abuse drugs. Adults and their children who engage in substance abuse generally feel lonely, isolated, frustrated, and have negative self-concepts. They typically have little sense of ethical values. This lack of self-esteem undoubtedly is a key contributor to their initial interest in drugs (Nobles et al., 1987).

The example that parents set clearly affects how their children act. Adolescents tend to use drugs if their parents do (Maddox, 1970; Smart and Fejer, 1972; Kandel, Kessler, and Margulies, 1978A, 1978B). The most important factor related to teenage drinking is not whether or how often either parent drinks, but how much they drink each time (Lawrence and

Vellerman, 1974). Teenagers who abuse alcohol are often following in the footsteps of their parents.

We need to examine more closely how family members in-
teract with each other, too, because the quality of personal relationships in the family makes a difference in whether children
use drugs. In families who abuse drugs, parents often reject their
children or have low expectations for their success (Braucht et
al., 1973; Oyemade, 1985). These parents often define rigid,
stereotyped sex roles for themselves and their children (Kandel
et al., 1978A, 1978B).

In addition, the style of discipline parents use clearly con-
tributes to the potential that children may abuse drugs. Parents
of drug abusers often use negative discipline measures that are
either extremely strict or too permissive (Braucht et al., 1973;
Kandel et al., 1978A, 1978B; Oyemade, 1985). They may exces-
sively dominate and control their children (Braucht et al., 1973;
Oyemade, 1985). Parents in these families often fight about discipline and other issues (Kandel et al., 1978a, 1978b; McBride,
1978). Similarly, it appears that children in authoritarian, re-
ward-and-punishment types of educational programs are more
likely to engage in drug abuse and other delinquent behaviors
(Schweinhart, Weikart, and Larner, 1986).

Studies have shown consistently that although authoritarian childrearing styles may appear effective with younger children (e.g., they are obedient), the full effects of this parenting/
teaching style are not realized until children are older (Hawkins,
Lesliner, and Catalano, 1985). Apparently, children raised in
authoritarian homes and schools are robbed of the opportunities
to make responsible choices on their own because the adults are
so controlling. They receive token, meaningless rewards—or
may not even be recognized—for a job well done. Thus they
never live with the logical consequences of their own behavior.

As a result of these practices, children are less likely to in-
ternalize most social values. They may find it difficult or impossible to function effectively in a society that offers many choices.
They may use drugs (or engage in other delinquent acts) to rebel
against authority or to escape from the excessive control of
adults.

What, then, can parents and teachers do to instill in children a sense of self-discipline, the value of human life, and the desire to succeed?

Positive Childrearing Styles

A variety of factors are typical in families whose children avoid substance abuse and other delinquent behaviors. Warm, positive relationships between family members typify these families. They usually share society's general values. They are also more likely to attend religious services (Oyemade and Washington, 1989).

Families are less likely to have children who abuse drugs if:

- household tasks are distributed among family members (Kandel et al., 1978A, 1978B).

- families have high aspirations for children's success (Oyemade, 1985), and

- there are strong kinship networks among the family (Oyemade, 1985).

Family pride in children's accomplishments may also be linked to children's prosocial behaviors (Oyemade and Washington, 1989).

Affectionate, supportive parent-child relationships may influence adolescents to avoid alcohol and drugs. These families appear to meet the children's emotional needs, and consequently children derive a great deal of satisfaction from their families.

One of the most important factors that seem to lead teenagers away from drug and alcohol abuse is the use of a reasoned, democratic parenting style (Braucht et al., 1973). Children may help set the rules and certainly understand why they are necessary. The rules are thus more likely to be internalized. Teenage achievers often come from homes where parents use positive discipline, nurture and supervise their children, and hold strong religious values (Oyemade, 1985).

Longitudinal research on the consequences of early childhood programs confirms that positive, child-centered interactions are likely to lead to more prosocial behavior, at least into adolescence. For example, the results of the Perry Preschool Program showed that preschool participants had lower rates of involvement with the legal system, lower arrest rates, and lower number of self-reported offenses (Berrueta-Clement et al., 1984). Children who had attended preschool were more likely to have completed high school and have higher grade point averages than those who had not been in preschool. Similar results have been found in a study in the Philadelphia schools (Copple, Cline, and Smith, 1987) and at the Syracuse University Family Development Research Program (Lally, Mangione, and Honig, 1987). Children benefit not only from what but how they are taught.

Positive approaches to childrearing are typified by a focus on cooperation and on guiding children to solve their own problems. Adults listen to children's concerns and interests and offer support when it is needed. Children in these homes and programs experience the logical natural consequences of their actions. Good early childhood programs already incorporate these techniques within their curricula.

Let us now turn to how specific attention can be given to drug-abuse prevention measures in working with young children and their families.

A Model Drug-Abuse Prevention Program

This discussion has concentrated on childrearing practices that tend to lead children toward or away from the use of illicit drugs. Of course, many other factors within the community and society also play a role, although not nearly as directly. Therefore, any program designed to assist families in their efforts to raise self-disciplined children must look at the context within which the families are living.

Few drug-abuse prevention programs address the most important childhood predictors of adolescent drug use. None directly address family functioning, such as childrearing skills, conduct disorders, aggressive or shy traits in children, or academic failure. These, then, are the critical components of an effective drug-abuse prevention program: the program must be targeted to young children and their families, and the program must address families' basic needs.

The Program Must Be Targeted to Young Children and Their Families

The root of drug abuse clearly lies in family childbearing practices and early childhood program teaching techniques. The first step, therefore, is to learn more about the families in the community who could be reached so that strategies can be designed to meet their needs. Program planners must learn to assess the following questions with the family and in an appropriate cultural context:

- Which parents are strict, too easy, or moderate in their discipline approach? How are these techniques affecting their children now?
- What are family management and communication styles (especially in families with antisocial and/or substance abusing parents)? Are there preschool or elementary children with conduct disorders and antisocial behaviors?
- What role do factors such as racism and classism play in the struggle with drugs? In parents' willingness to attend meetings?
- What causes stress for the families—poverty, isolation, crime, unemployment, lack of resources, or. . .?

Unless enough is known about the families to tailor the program to their needs, the program probably will never get off the ground.

The Program Must Address Families' Basic Needs

Effective early childhood programs such as Head Start already have a strong parent involvement component upon which to build expanded services in stress management, resource identification, family support, and family education.

Stress management. A primary prevention program must assist families in learning how to avoid stress, or at least in figuring out how to deal with its negative effects. For example, parents can begin to think of ways to eliminate or reduce problems, or think of other reactions to stressful situations. These skills will apply now, when their children are young, and will continue to be useful as children enter adolescence.

Resource identification. Target families may need to learn more about local, state, or federal agencies that can provide assistance ranging from nutrition to transportation to counseling. Again, effective programs already have a resource base from which to draw as needed.

Family support. Most early childhood educators see children's families at least once a day and can therefore address concerns individually as they arise. These informal chats frequently lead to opportunities for parents to build on their parenting skills as they watch skilled teachers in action or as they discuss an idea with staff.

In addition, bimonthly neighborhood meetings have been successful in a Washington, D.C., drug-abuse prevention program. Parents are encouraged to bring friends, relatives, and neighbors. Groups meet in convenient public buildings such as schools, churches, or community centers, and at times that are mutually agreeable. Films, discussions, and speakers are effective in sparking expanded social networks and giving participants a chance to grow in their ability to handle specific family-related issues (see Carter and Oyemade, 1990).

Family education. Without an intensive program to inform parents about the likely effects of different childrearing practices, the program simply is much less likely to work. The brief review of research here makes it clear that some practices are clearly more appropriate than others. A good drug-abuse prevention program can help parents learn how to develop skills in family management and consistent interaction, reinforce children's learning, and teach young children appropriate interpersonal skills.

Some parents will, of course, pick up on these discipline styles by watching teachers at work with their children. Most, however, can benefit from participation in groups. The topic of

TABLE 8
Family Characteristics That Affect Children's Use of Drugs

Drug abuse is more likely in these families:	*Drug abuse is less likely in these families:*
Family members feel lonely, isolated, frustrated.	Family members have warm, positive relationships.
Parents and children communicate poorly, particularly fathers and sons.	Parents are committed to education.
Parents demonstrate little sense of ethics.	Parents believe in society's general values.
Parents and children lack self-esteem.	Family attends religious services.
Parents drink heavily.	Household tasks are distributed among all family members.
Children feel rejected.	Families have high aspirations for children's success.
Parents have low expectations of children.	Strong kinship networks exist in the family.
Families follows rigid, stereotyped sex roles.	The family is proud of children's accomplishments.
Family management is inadequate.	Affectionate supportive parent-child relationships meet the child's emotional needs.
Parents excessively dominate and control their children.	Children derive a great deal of satisfaction from their families.
Parents use negative discipline measures (either extremely strict or too permissive).	Parents use a reasoned, democratic discipline style.
Adults fight about discipline and other issues.	

Source: Washington and Oyemade, 1989.

discipline is always of interest, so group leaders' efforts can focus on helping parents first become aware of their own child-rearing patterns and styles of interacting with children. More effective and positive alternatives can then be introduced in non-threatening ways so participants can gradually make changes in their family relationships. Staff can design a program specifically for the group, or adapt other programs such as STEP (Dinkmeyer, 1980) or PET (Gordon, 1979). Many parents will be faced with the need to reduce children's aggression or shyness and may find Spivak and Shure's (1978) problem-solving approach particularly effective for developing interpersonal skills.

What are the advantages of a drug-abuse prevention program for families of young children enrolled in groups?

- Healthy lifestyles and prevention of problems are emphasized.
- Families are assumed to be in control of their own lives.
- Programs are accessible and affordable.
- Families will realize a profound difference in their children's opportunities to become self-disciplined, successful individuals.

Working with Prenatally Substance-Exposed Infants

Head Start staff dealing with young children and their families should become familiar with the characteristics of risk status for Fetal Alcohol Syndrome, prenatal exposure to other drugs, and the identification of substance abuse problems in the family. They should be trained to discuss alcohol and other drug use history with the parents. As there is often denial, the staff should be trained to deal with both denial and evidence of guilt in the parent.

As the long-term behavioral effects of prenatal exposure to alcohol and other drugs have not been clearly documented, there is no typical profile of a drug exposed child. Characteristic behaviors include heightened response to internal and external stimuli, irritability, agitation, tremors, hyperactivity, speech and language delay, poor task organization and processing difficulties, problems related to attachment and separation, poor social and play skills, and motor development delays.

In trying to address their problem, there are two major strategies—training of staff and intervention with the parents—to make the postnatal environment more nurturing. In working with the child in the classroom, NAPARE (1989) recommends the following:

1. "At risk" children need a setting in which classroom materials and equipment can be removed to reduce stimuli or added to enrich the activity.

2. The "at risk" child needs assistance in self-organization which can be facilitated by interacting within an orderly, child-appropriate environment.

3. The "at risk" child requires more structure and classification within the environment than do other children, but all children are more successful, particularly at the beginning of the year, if their environment is constant and clear.

In working with parents whose children have been prenatally exposed to drugs, a key component is supporting the parent to receive professional treatment and counseling through community support services. Once the parent has enrolled in treatment, the parent component of the primary prevention program becomes a key to developing the interpersonal skills to provide the nurturing necessary to have positive developmental outcomes from the child.

Since we do not know the full range of the effects of prenatal substance exposure, we want to be careful not to stigmatize or prematurely label the child as drug exposed. Collins and Anderson (1991) emphasize that "prenatal exposure" is a condition, not a diagnosis. Indeed, Head Start should focus on the child's *current* behavior and the family's *current* involvement with substance abuse rather than attempting to identify whether children have been prenatally affected by harmful substances. Collins and Anderson provide detailed information on organizational resources and specific curricula and model programs that are suitable for work with Head Start populations.

A Curriculum Designed
for the Head Start Community

In one concrete approach to addressing the issue of substance abuse prevention, Carter and Oyemade (1990) teamed with the National Head Start Association to develop a "Model Substance Abuse Prevention Program" for Head Start families. It was funded by the Office for Substance Abuse Prevention and the curriculum, "Parents and Children Getting a Head Start Against Drugs" is now being implemented in Head Start programs in all fifty states.

The curriculum was designed especially for Head Start parents and children. It is culturally responsive and based on accepted principles of child development and family support. The program design is based on data gathered from minority scholars interested in Head Start (see Washington and Oyemade, 1987).

Development of the curriculum was guided by research that identified factors that place certain families at higher risk of substance abuse (e.g., poor communication, low self-esteem, inadequate family management, excessive drinking), and characteristics that would make drug abuse unlikely to occur in families (e.g., warm positive relationships, strong kinship networks, commitment to education, and reasoned democratic discipline style). (See Washington and Oyemade, 1989.)

Specific curriculum content focuses on factors such as drug information, self-esteem, communication skills, stress, drugs in the community, health issues, values and peer pressure, family management and relations, and developing support networks. The curriculum is culturally based, using a discussion/experiential approach as opposed to being didactic, and activities are based on knowledge about the specific culture. There are ten sessions with a variety of activities, including lectures, discussions, role playing, self-assessment, and puppet construction.

The program is divided into two parts, one for parents and one for children. Children's activities are center-based, and parent workshops take place concurrently with the children's program. This allows children and parents to address the same topics at the same time. Trainers' guides were developed for both the parents' and the children's curriculum.

The Trainer's Guide

The trainer's guide includes an overview of the problem and a section on how to develop effective training and facilitation skills. It contains the following ten modules:

1. Orientation
2. Self-esteem
3. Communication
4. Stress
5. All around the community
6. Health issues related to drug abuse
7. Values and peer pressure
8. We are family
9. Developing support groups
10. Appreciating our families

The Parent Curriculum

Parents receive specific information about drugs and take part in activities focused on self-esteem, communication, stress, health issues, values, peer pressure, family management and relations, and developing support networks. Parents learn about the effects of drug abuse on the family, as well as effective parenting and drug-abuse prevention skills.

The parent activity book contains modules similar to the trainer's guide, and includes the following material:

- Specific information about drugs and the problem of drug abuse with discussion guidelines for parents to use with their children when addressing the topic;
- Self-esteem and self-appraisal activities with guidelines for communicating with children and ways to enhance a child's self-concept;

- Stress issues including the special stresses associated with drug abuse and how to recognize and deal with stress in children;
- Community resources;
- Health issues related to drug abuse;
- The importance of exercise;
- Looking at values and peer pressure;
- The role of the family in combating drug abuse; and
- How to develop support groups.

The Children's Curriculum

Children's activities are meant to be a portion or module of a program's drug-abuse prevention efforts, not to serve as the entire curriculum. Thus the children's curriculum is integrated into regular classroom activities. Each concept presented to children includes recommendations for activities parents can perform at home. Children's fears about drugs and poisons (not solely illicit drugs) are addressed. Children listen to songs and stories about how to "say no to drugs." These topics and activities are interspersed throughout the curriculum rather than being concentrated in one or two concurrent sessions. Children also learn about self-esteem, dealing with anger and pain, accepting responsibility, becoming familiar with their communities, the importance of exercise, assertiveness, cooperation, and nutrition.

The children's activity book contains the following lessons:

- Telling stories
- "This is me" book
- It looks like candy
- I get so angry when . . . I drop my glass
- Our block
- Family exercise time
- No is a good word
- Family notes

- Mean words hurt
- It's good for you

Activities focus on discovering children's feelings about drugs; developing self-esteem; recognizing drugs and poisons; managing difficult feelings; taking responsibility for one's mistakes; learning about the community as a means of maintaining personal safety; the importance and fun of exercise, especially as a family activity; how to say "no" to things that make them uncomfortable; the "specialness" of families and the importance of family communication; dealing with feelings; the importance of good eating habits; and the relationship between good nutrition and health.

Impact of the Curriculum

A user survey has been distributed to determine the number of parents and children who have actually participated in the curriculum. Data to date indicates that more than 3,000 parents have been trained in the curriculum.

In general, participant evaluation of the substance abuse curriculum has been very positive. For example, at one site, the coordinator indicated, "Overall, the facilitators felt that those parents who attended the training were sorry to see it come to an end and they seemed to really benefit from its content. Comments were made by parents who changed their attitudes toward their children. In particular, the changes were in regard to discipline, showing affection and communication."

Experimental and control groups were also administered pre- and post-measures of several factors which were addressed in the curriculum. Preliminary results indicate that the experimental group showed significant gains in locus of control, parent health information, opinions about drugs, assertiveness skills, parenting skills, and drug knowledge. This suggests that the curriculum had a significant impact on the reduction of the family risk factors associated with substance abuse.

The development of the curriculum involved several phases. The first model program was implemented in Head Start programs in Baltimore, Maryland. It was then replicated by several regional affiliate groups of the National Head Start Association under the direction of a team of educational researchers. In accordance with the goal of prevention, these model programs were conducted in cities with high-risk populations of low-income, Hispanic, and black families. It was then replicated in other cities over several years.

Participant responses to early phases of the project were very enthusiastic, resulting in more than 500 requests for implementation at other Head Start sites throughout the country. In addition, Florida, Oregon, and Ohio are using the curriculum throughout their respective states. The many requests for presentation of this model revealed an apparent lack of available models for preschool programs. As the program continued, the curriculum was refined and developed so that it could be used on a national basis. Future revisions will incorporate more background information and follow-through techniques for the trainer's guide.

The final phase of the curriculum development focused on the training of potential trainers at each of the ten regional Head Start association meetings. These trainers were to then implement the program in their respective sites. The procedure, which served as a prototype for implementation, involved training twenty potential trainers of trainers (ten teacher trainers and ten parent trainers) from each region in the Head Start drug-abuse prevention trainer's program.

Subsequent to the training, the trainer-trainers provided training to parent-trainers and teacher-trainers at their sites. Approximately thirty persons participated in each session. More than fifty training sessions were conducted. Each Head Start program represented an average of a prospective 1,500 families to receive training. Individuals were trained from forty-nine states (excluding Hawaii), Puerto Rico, and the U.S. Virgin Islands.

In addition to the regional training programs, on-site technical assistance and training has been provided to more than fifty Head Start programs using a cluster and an individual site approach.

Conclusion

In summary, substance abuse is a persistent and increasing problem in Head Start programs. Head Start must address the problem from a proactive position of prevention and intervention. As a result, the following advantages of a drug-abuse prevention and intervention program for Head Start families and their children will be realized:

- Healthy life styles and prevention of problems will be emphasized.
- Families will assume control of their own lives.
- Programs will be accessible and affordable.
- Families will realize a profound difference in their children's opportunities to become self-disciplined, successful individuals.
- Teachers will be sensitized to the needs of prenatally drug exposed children.
- Children will not be stigmatized.
- The postnatal nurturing of the children by the family will be enhanced.
- Treatment of families will prevent further prenatal exposure.
- Effective and coordinated treatment will enhance the overall functioning of Head Start families.

CHAPTER 7

The Challenge of Involving Men

Fathers' Roles in Child Nurturance

Head Start parent involvement was originally conceived as serving three functions: education of parents in self-development and parenting skills, training of parents in decision making to enable parents to bring about institutional change, and increasing the employability of parents to improve buying power and income.

As more emphasis was placed on the education of parents for self-development and parenting skills, most parent involvement programs were oriented toward mothers of Head Start children. The small percentage of male participants has consisted of a few fathers, boyfriends, and grandfathers. Some of the reasons cited for low father involvement include: (1) lack of interest; (2) difficulty in seeing themselves as able to can teach their children; (3) in the case of African Americans, negative attitudes the general public has about African American men; (4) scheduling of activities at inappropriate times; (5) lack of male representation on Head Start staffs; (6) lack of activities that are male-oriented; and (7) lack of an intense effort to develop strategies that would increase their participation.

According to Lamb (1981), changes regarding men's roles in the family have been slow and, in many instances, completely ignored. Moreover, men who wish to assume a more active role in their families must contend with various institutional, economic, legal, and attitudinal barriers.

There is an obvious need for increasing father involvement in Head Start. Fathers, married or unmarried, play significant roles in the nurturance of children. In addition, they might benefit from personal development courses such as substance abuse prevention, family literacy, and other Head Start initiatives. Also, increased employability of fathers could greatly increase the financial support available to Head Start children. Further, father involvement in planning and policy could increase the men's roles and responsibilities in the community.

The father's role in child care and socialization has undergone changes. No longer are fathers exclusively responsible for the family's economic and material comfort. Mothers are increasingly entering the work force, and families are depending on the wages of both parents. However, as researchers have documented, maternal employment may be only one of many reasons for the father's increased role in the nurturance and socialization of children (McAdoo, 1981). John McAdoo (1981) suggests that fathers' increased interactions with their children may reflect their desire to have an increased part in the development of their children. Especially in African American families, fathers have been reported as providing significant child care and household task assistance (McAdoo, 1981). Indeed, a slightly greater percentage of African American households, compared to white households, consist of a male and his own children; there has been an 81 percent increase in African American male householders (no wife present) from 1980 to 1989 (for details, see Austin, 1992, p. 36).

Likewise, calls to increase participation in Head Start activities have had a similar increase. A common core of initiatives has been the "educative" approach. For example, in a study of fathers' participation in a parent education program to build communication skills, Levant and Doyle (1983) found an improvement in fathers' communication skills in terms of their overall sensitivity to their children's feelings and point of view. The authors also noted that fathers appeared to change their thinking about family relationships after participating in the program. A particularly important premise advanced by Levant and Doyle (1983) is that increasing men's involvement in the family could be facilitated by an educational intervention. This notion is obviously not new to Head Start programs, but reaching fathers and making them aware of the importance of their involvement have proven to be quite difficult.

Need to Focus on Supporting Male Employability

Perhaps one reason for the difficulty in involving men is the lack of relevance of parent involvement activities to men. A major concern in the lives of many Head Start fathers is obtaining a job or job skills. Given the dramatic increase in out of marriage childbearing and the consequent feminization of poverty, the perception of "deadbeat dads"—young unmarried fathers who are irresponsible, careless victimizers of young women and have little or no interest in their children—has become commonplace. Yet research has revealed that the situation of young fathers is much more complex than is suggested by this stereotype. For example, a recent report by the Children's Defense Fund based on evidence from a number of studies suggests that formal marriage and the payment of formal child support should not be the only measures of young fathers' willingness to parent.

Equally important, it is also clear than many young fathers are at a disadvantage in the labor market—they are disproportionately likely to have dropped out of school, to have low basic academic skills, and to have other problems. Further, CDF reports that young unmarried men and women are far less likely than in earlier decades to marry if the young women is pregnant. As pointed out in an earlier chapter, an increasing number of Head Start parents are teen mothers. One possible reason for the increase in unmarried teens is the declining economic prospects of young men, particularly poor and minority youths. Young men with adequate earnings are three to four times more likely to be married than their peers without adequate earnings (for details, see Austin, 1992).

Unmarried fathers, teens or adults, are most likely to be unemployed because they lack the educational credentials, basic academic skills, and employment experience needed to secure steady, well-paying jobs. Also, both groups are hampered further by the fact that they are more likely to have had suffered challenges such as having been suspended from school or involved in illegal activities which make it difficult to find employment. If not living with the mother of the child, young fathers are more likely to be living with relatives, which suggests that they may have difficulty in supporting a family.

This growing inability of young men to earn decent wages has taken its toll on young families in two ways. It has discouraged family formation and has reduced the chances that young families, whether headed by a young single mother or by a married couple, will escape poverty. Because young absent fathers are among the young men who have suffered the sharpest declines in their earning ability, they are unlikely to be able to provide substantial support. Consequently, more than four out of five young single mothers are poor. Furthermore, many young married couples are also poor.

While Head Start has been instrumental in increasing the employability of Head Start mothers, few training programs have been oriented toward occupations appealing to fathers. Head Start could be instrumental in improving the employability of young fathers.

Father Participation in Decision Making

Participation in decision making in Head Start takes the form of participation on the policy council, serving on boards, participating in political activities, and organizing community groups to bring about change in the community. Participation in these activities has been found to be associated with the upward mobility and empowerment of parents to bring about change in the community, as well as in their own lives.

Participation on policy councils has been dominated largely by Head Start mothers. Where fathers have participated, they have made significant contributions to the council. Further, participation has improved the image of lower-income males by portraying them as stable, responsible fathers. This has also increased the employability of some fathers by providing skills helpful in obtaining employment and being successful on the job. Moreover, participation by fathers in decision-making roles provides a positive role model for Head Start children, particularly male Head Start children.

Toward Increased Male Involvement

In the current Head Start program, participation in the parent involvement component is less than 10 percent male. Beatty (1989) reported that nearly three-fourths of the fathers reported that they participated in Head Start activities only a few times a year or not at all. When staff persons were asked which parent is more likely to participate in Head Start activities, no one chose fathers. Further, Beatty found that although almost all staff persons believed that parent/father involvement is important, a disturbing number of staff members expressed skepticism about the specific benefits of parent/father involvement in center and child activities.

Beatty asked mothers, fathers, and staff to rank in order the reasons for low father participation. Their responses are listed in Table 9.

Overall, four factors stood out in the poll as major contributions to the low rate of participation by fathers in Head Start programs. The first was the need for information. Everyone agreed that mothers did not tell fathers about, or encourage them to participate in, Head Start activities. This suggests that fathers did not know about the Head Start activities or the value of their participation in such activities.

It is also possible that the father's absence from the home, the second-highest-ranked reason given by mothers and staff, may be an acknowledgment of the difficulty of relaying information to the father.

The third problem addressed was the predominance of female staff and female-related activities. Additionally, the scheduling of activities at convenient times, particularly for fathers, had to be discussed.

It is also important to note that lack of interest or lack of ability on the part of the father was not cited as a major factor by any of the groups reporting—mothers, fathers, or staff.

TABLE 9

Ranking for Reasons for Low Father Participation

Reasons	Mothers	Fathers	Staff
Head Start staff is mostly female.	1	1	6
Father is absent from the home.	2	8	2
Activities are mostly female related.	3	2	8
Mothers don't tell fathers about the activities.	4	4	5
Mothers don't encourage fathers to be involved.	5	5	4
Fathers feel no need to be involved.	6	7	1
Head Start staff does not view father involvement as important.	7	6	14
Fathers are too impatient with children.	8	10	9
Fathers are not clear about what parent involvement entails.	9	9	4
Activities are at inconvenient times for fathers.	10	3	12
Fathers feel children are the mother's business.	11	10	3
Fathers don't know how to work with young children.	12	14	10
Fathers are uncomfortable with young children.	13	15	7
Fathers feel that children are the program's responsibility	14	12	11
Parent involvement program lacks clear supervision	15	11	17
Fathers are incapable of working with young children	16	15	13
Fathers are not interested in their children's education	17	16	15
Parent involvement program lacks clear goals and objectives	17	13	17
Fathers distrust Head Start staff	18	16	18
Head Start staff is unfriendly toward fathers	19	15	16

Source: Beatty, 1989.

Fathers cited inconvenience of time, activities being mostly female related, and the female gender of staff as the most important deterrents to participation.

Model Programs

In 1991, six Head Start programs received special grants to implement demonstration and research projects to increase male involvement. Here we report on two such programs: H.I.M. in Pinellas County, Florida, and Mercer County, New Jersey.

A Florida Initiative

In St. Petersburg (Pinellas County), Florida, a male involvement program targeting Head Start fathers and father figures provided workshops in interviewing/job readiness skills, literacy, college readiness, child development/discipline, substance abuse, interpersonal relations, cultural sensitivity, and other areas. Participants were also required to plan, budget, and execute a community service project. Response to the program was excellent.

The expected outcome of the program was that participants would gain in self-esteem, develop skills needed to cope with their environment, improve their employability, and improve their relationships with and understanding of their Head Start children and families. A special segment of the program dealt with measuring each participant's degree of influence on his own destiny at the beginning and end of the program.

Barriers to the program included transportation, child care, and the fact that some men were employed; arranging workshop hours required careful planning. A stipend was provided to assist with transportation and child care. At the opening retreat participants were asked to select the best hours and thereby increased their vestiture in maintaining their commitment to the program and attending workshops.

H.I.M. in New Jersey

In fall 1992, the *NHSA Journal* reported on the accomplishments of the Mercer County Head Start Child Development Program, Inc. in New Jersey for Project Head Start Involving Males (H.I.M.).

Consuelo B. McDaniel, executive director for twenty-six years, stated,

> As many times as I have entered a Head Start classroom, there has never been anything more heartwarming than the way a male's presence creates a magic moment, such as little boys greeting the males as 'Daddy' or seeing their excitement over the size and strength of the male when they say 'pick me up to reach the sky.' They immediately become attached and plead with the male to stay.
>
> These poignant scenes made me aware of the importance and obvious need of the male role model in these little children's lives. Therefore, Mercer County Head Start has designed Project H.I.M. as a means to help the male focus and identify his place as a role model in the lives of our children.

To increase male involvement, Project H.I.M. first addressed "negative attitudes and behaviors toward males." This was accomplished through male sensitivity training sessions for staff, parents, and numerous Region II and III Head Start and early childhood development programs.

The focus of these training sessions was to change some of the stereotypical views toward males and provide an avenue for dialogue to erase the assumption that males do not want to be involved in the development of their children. Strong emphasis was placed on showing males that their role and responsibilities go beyond just being the disciplinarian and breadwinner.

Making the male feel welcome in the classroom was also addressed. H.I.M. provided resources that included books, paintings, and photos to assist in changing the cosmetics of the classrooms. Showing males interacting with children in the classroom is a constant reminder to staff, parents, and children that male involvement is very important in the development of children.

Project H.I.M. provides workshops, information, and resources in seven priority areas:

- self-esteem,
- child development,
- parental legal rights and responsibilities,
- career enhancement,
- planned parenthood,
- continuing education and literacy, and
- general counseling.

To achieve these objectives, strong collaborations have developed with community agencies, influential individuals, and numerous funding sources including the New Jersey Nets, Coca-Cola, Pizza Hut, ShopRite Supermarkets, Microsoft, Jostens Learning, and Childcraft Education Corporation.

Project H.I.M. is based on several assumptions which are currently being tested. These assumptions are:

1. Male parents who participate in Project H.I.M. will become more informed about child development, parental legal rights and responsibilities, career enhancement, and planned parenthood.

2. Males who participate in Project H.I.M., will spend more time with their children.

3. Children whose parents participate in Project H.I.M. will benefit cognitively, socially, and emotionally.

4. Males who participate in Project H.I.M., as well as the mothers of Head Start children, will show increased levels of self-esteem.

5. Mercer County Head Start, as reflected through its policy council and through classroom volunteers, will have significantly more males involved in the Head Start program.

Even as the impact of Project H.I.M. is being tested, the initiative has already shown promising results. Some project accomplishments are as follows:

1. Through intensive involvement with families by the social service component, Project H.I.M. has identified 185
   male role models for 199 children. When there was no
   father or other male role model available, mothers were
   encouraged to find an appropriate male role model
   within their own family structure. As new children are
   recruited, relaying the importance of Project H.I.M. to
   the primary caretakers—who in most cases are single
   mothers, grandmothers, and legal guardians—continues
   to be a challenge for the family workers and staff of
   the project.

2. For the first time in twenty-six years of operation,
   Mercer County Head Start Child Development Program,
   Inc. has elected a male to serve as policy council chair-
   person. Of the eight parent representatives and four
   alternates, there are three male representatives and one
   male alternate.

3. After two months of the program, head teachers requested the recruitment of males to volunteer in the
   classrooms. This turnabout confirms the awareness of
   the education component and their understanding of the
   need and importance of providing male role models in
   the classrooms. Moreover, it is a notable change in attitude by the program staff. Subsequently, males became
   involved in every Head Start center, and a "Male
   Volunteer of the Month Award" was instituted for each
   center.

4. Project H.I.M. collaborated with the First Step Teen
   Fathers program on its Parent Fair Share, entitled
   "Operation Fatherhood," and funded through Man-
   power Development Research Corporation, to provide
   the program with fifteen male referrals to complete a
   twelve-week employment program.

5. Throughout the first year, H.I.M. networked with the
   Philadelphia Parent and Child Center Men's Club
   (another demonstration and research project) to sponsor
   a three-game basketball series at alternate sites.

6. Recognition was given to fathers and male role models through many activities during the week before Father's Day. "Father's Week" at each center included Fix-it Day, Career Day, another basketball tournament, Movie Night with males and significant others, and a male and child activity trip to Great Adventure Animal Safari. The highlight of the week was a banquet attended by 153 family members in recognition of Project H.I.M.

Recommendations

Both the Florida and New Jersey projects demonstrate that male involvement in Head Start can be increased with potential benefits for the entire family. To extend the lessons learned, given the overall low involvement of fathers, what can be done to increase father involvement?

Here are a few suggestions:

1. Review the expectations of the parent involvement component in view of parent needs and staff support and resources. It is likely some adjustments will have to be made.

2. Develop parent involvement programs that are more cognizant of not only male interests, but also child, family, and marketplace needs.

3. Conduct needs assessments by asking for continuous feedback from mothers and fathers. Initial family assessments are a good start, but progress should be continuous. Family assessments may mean two or more assessments for one child.

4. Develop more employability programs based on the interests of men associated with Head Start children.

5. Establish collaborative/cooperative relationships with other programs such as the federally funded Jobs Training Partnership Act (JTPA), which provides job training for males.

6. Include training which focuses on male-female/couples relationships.

7. Involve more men and community groups in Head Start operations as staff, advisors, or collaborators.

8. Provide greater support—preferably in higher pay—to Head Start staff.

PART C

*Issues for the
Twenty-First Century*

CHAPTER 8

Overview of Head Start Issues

Head Start approaches the twenty-first century more popular than ever, assured of its continuing existence, and facing many challenges. Chief among these challenges are:

- expansion issues
- staff development concerns
- research and evaluation questions

Each of these challenges relates to the realm of defining and assuring program quality, as will be evident from the following discussion.

Focus on Quality

Clearly, the decade of the 1990s will be remembered as the Head Start "quality time." Up until the 1990s, the requests for "full funding" of Head Start and the need to serve more than 15 percent of eligible children had been a staple on the child advocacy agenda for decades. The Head Start community watched enrollments drop below 400,000 between 1970 and 1982; between 1965 and 1969, enrollments were above 500,000 children. Since 1983, both enrollments and budgets have expanded rapidly: enrollments rose from 414,950 in 1983 to an estimated 721,268 in 1993. The budget nearly tripled in this time frame.

These rapid increases in budgets and enrollments have not occurred without cost, however. Not surprisingly, there has been energetic discussion about Head Start expansion, including criticism that program quality has declined. Obviously, reasonable people differ on how fast the program should grow and how best to assure quality outcomes for children and families.

The 1980s

Issues of program quality began to surface gradually as a result of Ronald Reagan's expansions of Head Start. Just prior to the period of rapid expansion, in FY 1982, President Reagan proposed that Head Start be repealed and placed in a block grant at significantly reduced funding levels, and that program regulations, including performance standards, should be streamlined. More than 5,000 letters were sent to the Reagan administration protesting those changes (CDF, 1985).

Then President Reagan, in an apparent policy reversal, included Head Start in his "social safety net," provided increased funding, and targeted increases to pupil enrollment. These increases were accompanied by severe cuts in other federal programs which provided direct support to Head Start programs (Washington and Oyemade, 1987, p. 81–84). Thousands of children were added to the programs between 1980 and 1984; in 1983, gains occurred despite no appropriations increase (Subcommittee on Human Resources, 1984). The Reagan administration estimated that the same number of children could be served in 1986 as in 1985 at the same funding level, which was an $80 million increase over 1984 (Stephan, 1986). The actual appropriation for 1986 was a $12 million increase.

Child advocates have argued for increased funding for Head Start so that a greater percentage of the eligible population can be served (only 15–18 percent are now being served). The administration argued that, with improved enrollment practices, a greater percentage of those eligible could be served. The administration also pointed out that in the past funds have been earmarked for expansion grants and that Head Start enrollment has improved as a result (Stephan, 1986).

Zigler and Lang (1983) argued that if expansion of Head Start would provide services to more children while preserving and upgrading the quality of current programs, "anyone who cares about children would be in favor of it" (p. 5). Adding that they doubt this would be the case, they stated that they would rather see fewer children served well than more children served poorly. "Tokenistic" efforts to serve children are dangerous, not so much because they damage children as that they give the appearance that something useful is being done and thus become a substitute for more meaningful efforts (Zigler and Valentine, 1979).

Thus, concern about the eroding quality of the comprehensive mandate began to be voiced. For example, in 1982, federal subsidies for meals and snacks served under the U.S. Department of Agriculture Child Care Food Program were reduced, a $20 million loss to Head Start that year (CDF, 1985). Despite the fact that in FY 1984, Congress rejected the administration's proposal to move the food funds directly into the Head Start budget and to deny the automatic adjustment, the administration re-proposed this plan for FY 1985 (CDF, 1984). Again, the proposed $80 million "increase" in Head Start funding effectively froze funds for food, resulting in about an $8.5 million loss to Head Start in 1984, the equivalent of slots for about 3,500 children (CDF, 1984).

Aside from budget cuts, administrative changes in the 1980s also affected the comprehensive mission. In the effort to "expand" Head Start through increased enrollment, programs which served children for only one year were scored higher in the grant process than programs which served children for two years. Again, this approach increased quantity at the expense of providing services for the neediest children. According to Clarence Hodges, former commissioner of the Administration on Children, Youth, and Families, "our problem is, if we had children that needed coats and we could give coats and sweaters to some, should we give coats to all or coats and sweaters to some?" Representative George Miller of California replied: "What concerns me is whether or not the coat you then give them keeps them from freezing to death" (Washington and Oyemade, 1987, p. 83).

The 1990s

In early 1990, President Bush demonstrated a strong commitment to Head Start by requesting a $500 million increase. On January 31 he said, "[Head Start] is something near and dear to all of us. . . . All [children are] special, because they are the very future of freedom." Throughout the spring and summer of 1990,

Congress moved forward a reauthorization bill that called for more than $7 billion by 1994 to serve all eligible children ages three to five (Human Services Reauthorization Act of 1990). President Bush almost doubled Head Start funding, increased the number of children served, and proposed in 1992 a further increase of $600 million—the largest one-year increase in its history. With that, the program could give almost all eligible children at least one year of Head Start (Besharov, 1992).

Similarly, President Clinton's FY 1994 budget sought to increase Head Start funding to $4.2 billion, an $874 million increase over the FY 1993 revised level, which included $500 million for summer Head Start as part of the president's economic stimulus package (Clinton, 1993). Under this Clinton proposal, expansion would include additional enrollment as well as quality enhancements. Some programs would expand from half-day to full-day programs, facilitating participation in Head Start for children from low-income families who work full time. The FY 1994 budget suggested $194 million in quality improvement funds, half of which would enhance teacher salaries; the remainder would be used for specific grantee needs such as improving facilities and equipment, transportation, and/or hiring additional staff. An estimated $81 million would be used to provide a cost-of-living increase to grantees, and $83 million would fund training and technical assistance activities.

Besharov (1993) points out that Clinton's now-extinct 1993 stimulus bill to spend $500 million for new summer programs sent Head Start offices into a planning frenzy. Even before the bill failed the Senate, it became apparent that many grantees would have difficulty switching to a year-round schedule. Some did not have the use of their classrooms over the summer and were having trouble finding alternate facilities.

According to NAEYC (1993), expansion efforts should be designed to ensure that high-quality Head Start experiences are provided to all new enrollees as well as those children already enrolled in the program. Current Head Start law requires that 25 percent of any new funds be used for quality improvements, with half of that amount targeted for improved compensation, and that 2 percent of overall funds be used for training and technical assistance. NAEYC supported the provision of quality set-asides. Simply enrolling more children to raise the percentage of eligible children served by Head Start without sufficient attention to ensuring high quality services is unacceptable.

NAEYC also urged that expansion be used to enhance Head Start's leadership role. In particular, NAEYC stressed the need for innovative models for serving infants and toddlers, including high-quality infant/toddler child care, parent-child home visiting programs, and family resource programs. NAEYC also viewed Head Start expansion as an opportunity for federal leadership in fostering greater collaboration among all types of services for young children and their families to promote the delivery of high quality, seamless services within the community. Because of the success of the model Head Start collaboration projects in fostering greater collaboration among all the various service providers for children and families at the state level, NAEYC recommended that expansion funds include provision for Head Start collaboration projects in every state.

According to the Inspector General's report (1993), during the three 1990–1991 Head Start increases of the Bush era, which totaled $425 million, 13 percent of grantees were unable to spend all of their funds; more than half of these had trouble finding or renovating facilities; around 50 percent had difficulty finding qualified staff; and more than 25 percent were unable to locate eligible children. As a result, they served 6 percent fewer children than had been financed. During the next wave of Bush increases, which added $502 million, 25 percent of grantees did not even apply for grants.

Expansion Issues

A number of specific concerns have been tied to the expansion and quality debate. These concerns include facilities, transportation, rising non-personnel costs, performance standards, the curriculum, administration, coordination of services, the need to serve new populations, and the need to continue experimentation with program options.

Facilities

Notably, the facilities issue was not apparent in the 1980 report to the president (HHS, 1980), but it is a big issue now in the 1990s. NHSA (1990) reports that over the past decade, Head Start programs have experienced a shortage of affordable and appropriate facilities. Due to an expanding preschool population, public schools have taken back space that they had given or rented to Head Start programs in the past (Goodman and Brady, 1988). This is most alarming since the General Accounting Office estimates that 29 percent of Head Start's facilities are located in public school buildings. Many landlords are no longer willing to donate space and in many cases are asking for commercial rates. One Massachusetts Head Start director reported that rent costs had increased 100 percent in 1989 (NHSA, 1990).

A survey by Mississippi Head Start directors found that 25 percent of the centers needed to be replaced (Moore, 1989). In some areas, rising costs for renovation serve as a disincentive to repair facilities, particularly when they are seen as temporary. Head Start centers located in old buildings often have outdated electrical wiring and heating equipment and appliances that are expensive to maintain (Hill, 1989). Further, many Head Start programs use portable buildings (which could be purchased as equipment). Obviously, these mobile Head Start units are much less stable than permanent buildings (CDF Reports, October 1992).

Lack of available space often affects a program's ability to expand services. New classrooms and parent rooms are scarce. Programs may be forced to run double sessions, reducing their ability to increase hours of operation, despite family needs (NHSA, 1990).

In 1992, Congress approved changes in Head Start that, for the first time, allowed local Head Start grantees to purchase buildings to house their programs (CDF Reports, October 1992). These changes recognize that Head Start is no longer just a demonstration project, but a permanent part of the nation's early childhood care and education system.

Transportation

The need for better facilities is matched by the demand to improve transportation systems. Transportation is often one of the most expensive items in the budget because of the rising costs to purchase and maintain vehicles and insurance, comply with state and local safety standards, and train and support staff. As a result of cutbacks in transportation systems, some grantees have narrowed the geographic area they serve or serve different types of families. This leads to decreased ability to serve many rural areas and to decreased use of home-based services, regardless of family needs. In addition, NHSA (1990) reports that parents' lack of transportation is a disincentive to parent involvement and a barrier to obtaining both medical services and job training opportunities.

Along with the ability to purchase facilities, in 1992, Congress also approved the development of minimum safety requirements for the purchase and operation of vehicles used by Head Start programs. According to Senator Edward Kennedy (D-MA), these safety regulations are critical because "many children in both rural and urban communities are transported in a range of vehicles every day" (CDF Reports , October 1992, p. 8).

Rising Non-personnel Costs

Finally, Head Start programs are experiencing rising costs in such non-personnel items as insurance, utilities, and telephone service. One Head Start program reported that over the past five years, they received a 12 percent increase in federal funds, an average of 2.4 percent a year; yet non-personnel costs increased by 46 percent over the same five years (NHSA, 1990).

Performance Standards

The Inspector General (1993) argues, essentially, that many Head Start programs are not meeting performance standards in critical areas, such as immunizations. In contrast, programs argue that there are significant differences between the reporting requirements and the standards. Since the early 1970s, the Head Start program performance standards have provided a guide to program implementation. Although a comprehensive revision of the performance standards was drafted in the late 1970s, and recommended for implementation in the 1980 report to the president (HHS, 1980), these revisions were never implemented. This is particularly troubling given the incorporation of new settings such as home-based services and programs serving younger children (NHSA, 1990).

Curriculum

Some argue that Head Start learning environments are poorly conceived and delivered in terms of *content*, while being stronger in nurturance. NHSA (1990) reports that there are several indications that a renewed effort should be made to ensure developmentally appropriate and culturally responsive practices in Head Start education services. This effort results from several factors:

- New knowledge regarding developmentally appropriate practice.
- The repeated need for Head Start classroom practices to be responsive to increasing cultural and linguistic diversity.
- The increasing concern over inappropriate child assessment and lack of clarity and guidance on this issue.
- The increases in group size and in the number of younger children.
- The need for new methods to work with special needs children, particularly those exposed to drugs or homelessness.

Administration

Administration is the most neglected aspect of quality. Dollars that go to management are sometimes perceived as taking money away from the children. NHSA (1990) reports that the administrative oversight of Head Start has been an area of concern for the past decade. The 1980 report to the president (HHS, 1980) found that the number of national and regional office staff had declined considerably since 1970 despite the program growth. In addition, the report found that regional office staff needed training in child development, and additional travel funds. It concluded that, at the national and regional levels, Head Start should be given the resources necessary "to administer a program of its stature." It is of serious concern that this situation appears to have continued unchanged (and perhaps has worsened) a decade after this finding was presented.

Coordination of Services

Head Start is a major catalyst for change and services to children within a network of many other services. There is a continuing need to focus on building linkages between Head Start and public schools, other early childhood and human service providers, the business community, and alternate service delivery models.

Public Schools

There is increasing concern that the progress made by children in the Head Start program may be lost when there is not continuation of comprehensive services in the school. At the federal and local levels, there has been a general lack of collaboration between Head Start and federal programs serving low-income families such as Chapter 1 and Follow Through (Advisory Committee on Head Start Quality and Expansion, 1993).

Head Start "transition projects" are currently being implemented in many locations throughout the United States (E. Kennedy, 1993). Like other school transition projects (for example, see "Success for All" as reported in Slavin et al., 1992, 1993), Head Start transition projects emphasize continuity between prekindergarten and family support services and always involve partnerships between a Head Start project and elementary schools.

One way to achieve better transition services to children would be to commingle funds for Head Start and Chapter 1 for children aged four to nine, focusing resources in schools serving the largest number of children in poverty (Zigler and Styfco, 1993). For example, Success for All prekindergartens are typically district-funded (usually from Chapter 1 or state compensatory education funds) (E. Kennedy, 1993).

Other Early Childhood and Human Service Providers

When Head Start began in the 1960s, it was most often the only early childhood program in a community. Today, in communities across the country, more and more early childhood programs have emerged. Although Head Start usually still provides the most comprehensive service available to low-income young children in many communities, today Head Start may compete with other early childhood programs for children, staff, and space. New funding streams are also now available to Head Start programs to expand services.

To address the need for linkages, in 1993 the National Head Start Association began its "Partnership Project" with funding from the W.K. Kellogg Foundation and the Ford Foundation. This project is expected to increase local collaborative efforts with public schools, child care programs, health providers, family support services, special needs services, and the private sector. The project will use five basic strategies to achieve this goal:

- Kellogg leadership institutes will include training, networking, and support of state Head Start association presidents on issues related to linkages in key areas.

- Technical assistance will include follow-up to state leaders and local Head Start communities to promote collaboration.

- A series of publications will be developed to document promising collaborative initiatives.

- Challenge grants will be provided to a limited number of Head Start programs to stimulate new collaborative efforts.

- National networking will include outreach efforts and partnerships with other national organizations.

The Business Community

The landmark report by the Committee for Economic Development, *Children in Need* (CED, 1987), recommended that business become a driving force in the community on behalf of public education and a prime advocate of educational initiatives for disadvantaged children. There is a desire for business involvement in promoting and investing in local Head Start programs and for sharing their management expertise with the Head Start community (see NHSA, 1990).

Need for Multiple Years of Service

Despite the need for flexibility to serve younger children, and legislative provisions that allow younger children and multiple years of service, recent Head Start policy seems focused on providing only one year of service for four year olds. This has been suggested as a way of targeting limited resources and reaching a higher percentage of the eligible population (with eligibility defined as four year olds). Moreover, Head Start staff report that they often need two years to provide the benefits reported by quality early childhood programs. This is especially true when serving multiple-problem families. Staff report that it often takes the entire first year to get to know the children and parents well enough to provide effective services. Similarly, for children whose primary language is not English, a segment of the Head Start population that has grown over the years, the second year is often critical.

Need to Serve Younger Children

NHSA reports serious concerns over this narrow definition of eligibility and the trend toward limiting multiple years of Head Start service. Head Start staff and parents speak of the critical need to serve three year olds, toddlers, and infants. The potential for promoting healthy development, reducing infant morbidity, intervening with teenage parents, and filling the gap in services to very young children with handicapping conditions all point to the need to expand Head Start services to this age group. Further, the need for Head Start services for very young children is reinforced by the growing number of Head Start parents in the work force or in new training programs. Most states are requiring participation in new welfare reform programs for mothers with children age three and over. Lack of adequate care for these very young children may place them at further risk if they spend multiple years in poor and inconsistent programs that do not provide the comprehensive services critical to low-income children.

Need to Continue Experimentation with Program Options

Greater experimentation is also encouraged through program options such as parent-child centers, family day care options, and full-day programs. The majority of Head Start services are now provided in center-based or home-based programs. Over the years, Head Start has successfully developed other models of service delivery, including the Parent and Child Centers (PCC) and the Child and Family Resource Program (CFRP), both of which could serve as potential program options. Currently, thirty-eight PCCs serve children under age three and focus on parent-child interactions. However, this option is not open to other Head Start programs. CFRP was a highly successful demonstration program launched in the 1970s that served the total family and focused on children from birth through age eight. Head Start no longer funds this demonstration.

In addition to these possible options, there are at least two dozen Head Start family day care programs. Although there has yet to be a national demonstration and evaluation of this model, such a family setting has great potential as the program moves to serve younger children, additional children under particular stress, and working parents (NHSA, 1990).

Finally, Head Start has always encouraged local innovation. However, there are no formal criteria or procedures that guide programs which seek to develop a locally designed option.

At a time when programs need a variety of alternatives, yet need to maintain program standards, additional guidance for the development of such services is critical.

Need for Full-Day Services

According to an HHS information memorandum (dated January 19, 1990), current Head Start policy states that funds can be used for full-day services only to children who need these services because they:

- have special needs,
- are from homes where stress due to factors such as seriously ill or emotionally disturbed parents is so great that full-day care for the child is essential, and
- have no care given at home because parents are employed in job training.

Despite this written policy, which basically allows full-day Head Start, programs are not encouraged to provide such services using Head Start funds. Instead, they are encouraged to seek and make maximum use of non-Head Start resources for financing full-day services. According to the Congressional Research Service (1990), a 1988 HHS study found that in some cases grantees were required to discontinue their full-day programs and convert them to part day (See NHSA, 1990).

Due to the needs of families however, many Head Start agencies have become involved in efforts to provide or broker child care services needed in the community. To do this they often enter into collaborative arrangements with other local programs and become involved in the use of other resources. "Wrap-around funding" is a term frequently used for this combination of Head Start funds with other federal, state, or local funds to extend Head Start services. The source of such funds may be state social services block grants, JTPA, work/welfare, parent fees, or other mechanisms such as seeking funds from private foundations.

For example, with a grant from the Kellogg Foundation in south central Michigan the local Head Start program is creating licensed day care homes to provide a continuum of high quality care for 180 children. The Michigan project targets families whose income level qualifies them to receive Head Start services (offered half days) for their preschool children but does not make them eligible for additional child care through department of social services funding. The child care providers participate in training with Head Start teachers, including CDA certification. This project benefits (1) the enrolled children, who receive a continuum of safe, positive care; (2) the parents, who will be able to pursue work or further education without the fear of leaving their children in less than satisfactory situations; (3) the child care providers, who receive regular employment, as well as education and training.

NHSA (1990) reports that Head Start directors are faced with complicated, time-consuming decisions about enrollment policies, cost allocations, and the establishment of fees for services. Although wrap-around funds allow programs to extend hours as well as provide linkages with other programs, a survey conducted by the National Head Start Directors Association (1989) indicated a number of disadvantages associated with "wrap-around," including:

- inadequate funds to maintain Head Start standards,
- conflicting regulations and eligibility and fiscal requirements,
- uncertainty of continual funding, and
- bookkeeping problems and additional paperwork associated with multiple funding sources.

Grantees depending on social service block grant funds say that it limits their ability to provide comprehensive services and that they could do much more for families if they were fully funded by Head Start. Other practical problems faced by programs interested in providing full-day services include space availability, moving from a school calendar to a full year, and a range of staffing issues.

While wrap-around funding has taken a priority role in Head Start strategic planning for the future of full-day Head Start, the National Head Start Directors Association has expressed concern that little has been done to actually define wrap-

Similarly, Schorr (1989) found these ingredients for success:

- Staff have the time, training, and skills necessary to build relationships of trust and respect with children and families,
- Staff deal with the child as part of a family, and the family as part of a neighborhood and community, and
- Programs cross long-standing professional and bureaucratic boundaries.

Clearly, well-qualified staff has emerged as the most important ingredient to program success. The National Child Care Staffing Study (Whitebook, Howes, and Phillips, 1989) documents the effects of the staffing crisis on the recruitment and retention of staff, and consequently on the quality of care.

Compensation

The National Head Start Association (1990) cites data which clearly illustrate the severity of the compensation issue:

- Forty-seven percent of Head Start teachers earn less than $10,000 per year. The average annual beginning salary of a Head Start teacher with a bachelor's degree in early childhood education in 1988 was $11,518 (63 percent of a beginning public school kindergarten teacher's salary). The overall average salary of a Head Start teacher was $12,074 (ACYF, 1988; see Collins, 1990).
- The non-teaching staff in Head Start also have low average salaries. Lewis (1988) indicates the national averages as follows:

    Coordinators:
Education	$15,034
Health	$13,487
Parent Involvement	$13,216
Social Services	$14,758
Social Service/Parent Involvement	$13,540

around funding and to explore or resolve the variety of issue
facing programs.

Staff Development Concerns

Many recent studies have reported that the quality of ea
childhood programs is affected negatively by staffing issu
Chief among these staffing issues are the interrelationsh
among staff recruitment and retention, training opportunit
and compensation (NHSA, 1990; Whitebook, Howes,
Phillips, 1989). New opportunities for women and poor com
sation in the early childhood field combine to create severe
shortages.

Head Start is not immune to these challenges. One c
most frequently mentioned concerns in an NHSA report (19
the deleterious effects of inadequate salaries and benefits c
recruitment and retention of staff. Indeed, this issue has su
repeatedly over the past decade, as many Head Start emp
have not had such standard employee protections as hea
surance and retirement benefits.

The Importance of Staff to Quality Programs

Many early childhood professionals cite the impor
staff to program quality. David Weikart (1989) cites the fc
among effective early childhood program characteristics

- At least two adults for each group of sixteen t
  preschool children,
- Staff trained in early childhood education, ar
  plan for continued inservice training and s
  classroom supervision in curriculum methodol
- Effective procedures that help staff observe e
  responses to the environment and the progran
- Good administrative backup, and
- Active involvement of parents in developing
  ating the program, and in parent training acti

Aides:
Health $ 8,311
Social Service/Parent Involvement $ 8,692

NHSA states that these low salaries often force Head Start staff (many of whom are women and former Head Start parents) to live in or near poverty, without critical benefits. Programs often cannot recruit trained staff, lose qualified staff, suffer low morale, and experience increased turnover. This situation becomes acute when public schools open new preschool programs offering higher salaries and draining qualified staff from Head Start. This turnover negatively affects the important trust relationship between Head Start programs and the children and parents served.

Head Start has taken significant steps to increase teacher salaries. For example, the 1990 Head Start reauthorization mandated that 25 percent of funds be spent on quality enhancements, with half of this earmarked for salaries.

Training and Technical Assistance

Clearly, Head Start programs have generally had greater access to training and technical assistance than many other early childhood programs. The Head Start Training and Technical Assistance (T/TA) network has played an important role in program quality.

The concept of community involvement has obviously led to strong feelings of affiliation within the Head Start network. Many Head Start advocates have been concerned that this broad communication network was threatened by two administrative changes in Head Start in the 1980s (Stephan, 1986):

1. Beginning in 1982, ACYF began to decentralize the training and technical assistance delivery system.

2. In 1985, the Reagan administration allowed the funding of the four bilingual/multicultural resource centers that had operated since 1978 to expire. Funding was instead provided to twenty-eight local groups.

Stephan notes that those opposed to decentralizing T/TA are concerned about jeopardizing the quality of training. In a related concern, the National Head Start Association identified reduced monitoring and training visits from regional offices as a major issue of the 1980s.

Further, reductions or changes in Training/Technical Assistance potentially limit parent involvement. One Head Start director testified before Congress that T/TA reductions prevented the program from providing mileage and babysitting reimbursements, thereby making it more difficult to maintain the parent involvement component (Roman, 1982).

Since Head Start is heavily dependent on parent volunteers, a reduction in T/TA is of serious consequence. Despite recommending an overall increase in Head Start funding for FY 1984, the Reagan administration also proposed a 50 percent cut in the portion of the Head Start budget targeted to training, technical assistance, research, demonstration projects, and evaluation. Since the Title XX training program was eliminated in FY 1982, there is no available substitute source of federal funding to meet the training needs of Head Start (CDF, 1984).

The Children's Defense Fund (1984) reports that in 1983, Congress directed the administration not to cut back on Head Start's research and training activities. However, this mandate was ignored.

Currently, ACYF funds a network of regional training centers and resource access projects that provide support to grantees. Grantees also receive direct funds for training.

The training and technical assistance network provides a range of services that include on-site training designed to meet the specific needs of individual programs; training grantees in priority areas, including services to handicapped children; extra training and technical assistance to high priority grantees; personal technical assistance; newsletters and other resource material; and cluster training on current issues (NHSA, 1990).

Nevertheless, Head Start training funds have not kept up with expansion. Moreover, the training network has at times suffered from disruption in service and changes in the delivery system. In fiscal year 1990, Head Start spent $30.6 million on training and technical assistance (HHS, 1990). However, as a percentage of total budget, Head Start training funds have decreased since 1974 (NHSA, 1990).

Declines in training funds are particularly deleterious in the context of staff turnover and the constant need to hire new staff. Critical supplementary support has been provided by the private sector. For example,

- Private sector collaboration efforts with Head Start include a major grant from the Johnson & Johnson Corporation to provide advanced management training to local Head Start directors.
- An Ad Council initiative urges private corporations to more actively promote and participate in Head Start.

Effective inservice education is a complex affair requiring more than isolated "one shot" training efforts. Inservice that assists participants to change must be relevant to their needs, be conducted by effective instructors, be supported by agency administrators and fellow staff members, include opportunities to observe and practice what is presented, and be accompanied by follow-up efforts which engage and involve participants. Future practice should emphasize and allow for this complexity. This will mean emphasizing and augmenting current efforts in a variety of ways.

- Inservice practitioners should conduct needs assessments that genuinely reflect the concerns and growth needs of participants—not of administrators speaking for their staffs. Needs assessment should be ongoing and designed to reflect changing training needs—not a yearly exercise for completing training plans.
- Inservice practitioners must ensure that administrators understand and endorse what is being presented and have a commitment to supporting change efforts on the job.
- Practitioners need to move beyond standard lecture formats and include time within the inservice for observation and practice opportunities which closely simulate the work setting. This will mean longer, more intensive workshops.

- Inservice should include discussion among participants for the purposes of deciding what to do and sharing ideas about how to do it.

- Staff development practitioners must highlight important points from the inservice on handouts and in resources for use and reference following the training.

- Practitioners must prepare themselves to conduct inservice, be knowledgeable about the subject, and show enthusiasm for the topic.

- Finally, practitioners and administrators need to include follow-up as an integral part of the inservice delivery system. This might mean conducting follow-up meetings, on-site visitations, or follow-up training sessions.

Research and Evaluation Questions

In addition to expansion issues and staff development concerns, a third major challenge for Head Start in the twenty-first century concerns research and evaluation questions. In the context of Head Start expansion, past research has demonstrated that quality programs for young children and their families can significantly improve their life course. Yet too little is known about the extent to which, and by what means, Head Start maximizes the potential of different types of children and families, and how future public policy can chart a course toward that end. More specific research on children and families is needed to answer these questions. Yet over the past fifteen years, the percentage of the Head Start budget devoted to research, demonstration, and evaluation (RDE) has decreased. In 1974, 2.5 percent of the overall budget was used for research and experimentation; in 1989, only .11 percent of the total budget was devoted to RDE activities. Current Head Start policy is primarily based on research conducted on programs designed many years ago. As problems faced by children and families change, there is a need for a new wave of research to inform decision makers on current policy issues.

Further, although Head Start has continued to be a leader in launching local innovations in response to current issues facing children and families, there have been few coordinated and systematic efforts to disseminate what has been learned from such innovation either within the Head Start community or in the larger early childhood and human service field.

Head Start Effectiveness: A Critical Assessment

Although Head Start's comprehensive design and emphasis on the "whole child" and parent involvement set it apart as a clearly unique program, the effectiveness of the education component has been the focus of public debate. Debate about whether Head Start "works" has generally been targeted at the program's academic benefits, undermining the value of the other program components.

The measurement of Head Start's effectiveness has been complicated by several factors. The scope and breadth of the program have made it more difficult to assess than other social programs. Indeed, as Valentine, Ross, and Zigler (1979) observed, Head Start's comprehensive program was characterized by several factors, including a multiplicity of goals which were to be accorded equal emphasis; the absence of clearly defined approaches for achieving each goal; the absence of a prioritized sequence of goal emphasis; and the built-in flexibility for programs nationwide to implement the program to suit the individual needs of the host community. These factors hindered both the achievement of any single aim and the evaluation of program effectiveness. To complicate the matter further, there was no reliable and valid instrumentation for evaluation by program personnel (Gordon, 1979). As a consequence, there was a rush to develop instrumentation overnight. Against this background, it is not surprising that Head Start's effectiveness has been questioned.

Yet there are several issues about which an assessment of Head Start must be concerned. Chief among these concerns has been the over-concentration of evaluative efforts on the use of IQ and other standardized tests when assessing the effects of intervention, the narrow focus on children's cognitive and intellectual

gains, the matter of appropriate definition and assessment of social competencies, and the underrepresentation of people of
color on committees that set and recommend policies bearing on
these matters. The latter concern is especially critical, given the
large proportion of children of color enrolled in Head Start and
the apparent concomitant underrepresentation of people of color
as teachers and senior staff in Head Start programs (Royster et
al., 1978).

Reports of Head Start Effectiveness Before 1990

Zigler and Rescorla (1985) report that strong evaluation
efforts were not part of Head Start's initial planning. An evaluation of the 1965 summer Head Start effort consisted of a hodge-
podge of instruments culled from the literature. This created
a strong negative reaction among Head Start staff and families
and led to inadequate and inconclusive results. Yet Head Start
enjoyed good press and became a major social program the
following year.

The Westinghouse report (Westinghouse Learning
Corporation, 1969) was the first large-scale national study to
evaluate the impact of Head Start participation on later school
achievement. Aside from a slight but significant superiority of
full-year Head Start children on some measures of cognitive and
affective development, the Westinghouse study concluded that
Head Start children were not appreciably different from their
non-Head Start peers in most aspects of cognitive and affective
development. Among the nine major findings of the Westinghouse report, the most positive dealt with the parents' strong
approval of the program and its effect on their children rather
than on measurable cognitive gains or social-emotional development (Steiner, 1976). The most publicized finding was that Head
Start showed only modest immediate gains on standardized tests
of cognitive ability and that these gains disappeared after the
first few years of elementary school. The Westinghouse report
also made an important recommendation: short summer programs in Head Start should be replaced with programs of longer
duration.

Steiner (1976) reported that responses to the Westinghouse study were mixed. While Nixon's public support of Head Start was apparently stifled by the study, in Congress, the Westinghouse study produced very little reaction and "no thoughtful reaction at all" (Steiner, 1976, p. 33). On the other hand, researchers produced several volumes of criticisms of the study's methods and findings (Smith, M.S., and Bissell, 1970; Campbell and Erlebacher, 1970A; 1970B; Bronfenbrenner, 1979B).

A few months after the release of the Westinghouse study, the federal Head Start administrative agency published its review of all Head Start research and evaluation conducted between 1965 and 1969 (Grotberg, 1969). That assessment concluded that Head Start children did not lose what they gained from the experience, but that they tended to level off at a plateau which allowed other children to catch up with them. Parental approval of Project Head Start was also confirmed; indeed, the children of parents who had a high level of participation performed better on achievement and developmental tests (Steiner, 1976).

Another major evaluation of Head Start was more optimistic. Early in the 1970s, Kirschner Associates (1970), evaluating Head Start's impact in local communities, illustrated that Head Start was an important social force in American society, Kirschner recorded 1,496 institutional changes in fifty-eight communities with full-year Head Start programs grouped into four categories. The four categories of the changes were: increased involvement of the poor at decision-making levels; greater employment of the poor as paraprofessionals; greater educational emphasis on the educational needs of the poor and minorities; and modification of health services and practices to serve the poor better and more sensitively. The Kirschner report concluded that Head Start effectively made local institutions more responsive to the poor.

In 1977, another federally sponsored review of Head Start research since 1969 was published (Mann, Harrell, and Hurt, 1977). This assessment of numerous evaluations of on-site Head Start studies confirmed that Head Start graduates: (1) enter primary school close to or at national norms on measures of school readiness; (2) maintain this advantage during the first year of school; and (3) fail to show substantially better performance in comparison with non-Head Start participants in grades two and three.

As will be seen later, results from longer term follow-up studies, which began to appear around 1979, show that Head Start graduates were less likely to be placed in special education classes or retained in a grade. Also, Datta (1979) reports that there are some "sleeper effects" on attitudes and achievement measures relative to non-Head Start comparison groups, but final levels of test performance are still woefully low for both groups.

A study by the General Accounting Office (GAO; 1979) reviewed the need for and impact of early childhood development programs on low-income families. GAO concluded that preschool programs that reach children during their first four years help them "perform significantly better in school" and produce "lasting, significant gains."

In contrasting these reports with the Westinghouse study, Steiner (1979) concluded that in the 1970s, Head Start had reached a standoff. The project remained popular among participants and acceptable to Congress. If it seemed not to be accomplishing lasting academic outcomes, its defenders argued that it accomplished other, nonacademic objectives.

Many of the bases on which the Westinghouse study has been criticized apply to findings from other national impact studies as well. These studies have been the focus of five primary criticisms:

1. *The narrowness of their outcome measures*: A commonly held misconception about Head Start is based on the idea that its primary purpose is to develop the cognitive capabilities and improve the IQs of disadvantaged preschool children (Richmond, Stipek, and Zigler, 1979; Gordon, 1979). For example, Wesley Becker (1981) asserted that the true goal of Head Start is to increase the IQ and school achievement of disadvantaged children; since initial gains in these areas "faded out," it could be concluded that Head Start was a failure. Nevertheless, as has been noted, Head Start has been since its inception a comprehensive program to improve health, nutrition,

social skills, and parents' involvement in their children's activities.

Zigler and Anderson (1979) decry the minimal attention devoted to the parent involvement component and the comprehensive "whole child" approach in assessments of Head Start, and observe that apparently it was easier to give children IQ tests than to find out if they were healthy and happy, or if their parents participated in the programs. Further, IQ tests are well-developed instruments that have proved valid and reliable predictors of school performance, whereas measures of social-emotional variables are few in number and not well understood (Richmond, Stipek, and Zigler, 1979; Zigler and Rescorla, 1985).

2. *Possible selection biases in who attended Head Start itself*: The issue of selection bias is important in interpreting evaluation results where randomly selected control groups are not available. As Datta (1979) explains, if one assumes that Head Start serves the neediest children first, the Westinghouse data reveal reliable and important value-added effects of Project Head Start on later achievement. Shipman's (1972) analysis of the data gathered for the 1969–70 national impact study demonstrates that Head Start clearly enrolls "least-advantaged" children. If generalizable, the Shipman data indicate that Head Start has reached out to children who are likely to have greater developmental lags than Head Start-eligible children who do not enter the program.

3. *The question of program continuity*: Relative to the question of program continuity, the issue is whether the special attention received by Head Start participants should be carried through to the primary school setting. Weisberg and Haney (1977) reviewed percentile ranks on the Mathematics Achievement Test (MAT) annually from kindergarten to third grade for the same pupils and found that at each readiness level, Head Start children who continued in Follow Through had steadier and higher performance than those who did not continue.

Stipek, Valentine, and Zigler (1979) argue that the idea that a one-shot preschool intervention can counterbalance the debilitating effects of inadequate inner city school systems and the associated conditions of living in poverty must be subjected to intense scrutiny.

4. *The failure to examine the effect of different curricula*: Another issue raised by the national impact studies is the effect of different curricula. A frequent criticism of the Westinghouse study was that it failed to examine differences in both the nature and quality of either the Head Start programs or the elementary school classrooms as factors influencing children's performance (Datta, 1979). This would seem to be a critical variable that must be examined, given Zigler's (1979) observation that there is likely to be as much variation within Head Start as there is between Head Start and non-Head Start environments. Mann et al. (1977) report data from Featherstone, who investigated whether planned variation in eight Head Start programs had differing cognitive effects on different kinds of children. Based on analysis of the first two years of planned variation, there is no one approach that will work for all children. Similarly, both Shipman and Zigler argue against the view that poor children are a homogeneous group universally in need of a single type of intervention program.

5. *The failure to examine the role of family process variables*: The final major issue identified by Datta is the role of family process variables. Datta reports that parents' formal schooling and the mother's educational aspirations and expectations for the child predict subsequent school performance. Dunteman et al. (1972) and Coulson (1972) report similar findings for the immediate effects of Head Start. Sally Ryan (1974) asserts that when parents are significantly involved in the project, gains can be maintained.

Head Start, according to Zigler and Anderson (1979), was designed to influence a broad array of factors including children's physical well-being, formal cognitive development, more circumscribed academic achievement, and socioemotional development. Zigler and Anderson warned that no one of these factors should be judged as preeminent; rather, all should be viewed as interacting in order to enhance social competence.

In the mid-1980s, the CSR, Inc., review of Head Start research, commonly referred to as the Head Start Synthesis Project, was published (see McKey et al., 1985, Stephan, 1986). This review compiled a bibliography of 1,600 documents (all published and unpublished Head Start research). The Head Start Synthesis Project concluded that:

1. The studies were "virtually unanimous" in finding that Head Start has immediate positive effects on children's cognitive ability but that the cognitive test score gains do not appear to persist over the long term (two years after Head Start).

2. Based on "very few studies," Head Start appears to affect the long-term school achievement of participants in terms of being retained in grade or assigned to special education classes.

3. There were immediate socioemotional gains in the areas of self-esteem, achievement motivation, and social behavior, with mixed results in the persistence of these gains over the long term (up to three years after Head Start).

4. There were positive findings in the areas of improved child health, motor development, nutrition, and dental care, but mixed results on whether the home diets of the children were better than those of non-Head Start children.

5. There were no significant differences in the health practices at home between Head Start and non-Head Start parents.

6. It was unclear whether parental involvement in Head Start is related to their children's cognitive test scores or whether Head Start improves parental childrearing practices.

7. Whereas anecdotal data indicated that Head Start improves the lives of many Head Start parents, no systematic research has been conducted on this topic.

8. Consistent with the Kirschner (1970) findings, CSR found that Head Start generated increased use of education, health, and social services, and that Head Start programs serve linking and coordinating roles with such services.

Head Start Evaluations: Lessons Learned for the 1990s

The U.S. Department of Health and Human Services convened in 1989–1990 an advisory panel for the Head Start Evaluation Design Project. This fifteen-member panel of national experts presented the first opportunity in more than a decade and a half for a systematic analysis of research needs relevant to the future of Head Start.

A Blueprint for the Future lists eight principles formulated by the panel:

1. Head Start research and evaluation planning should be organized around two principal questions:
   - Which Head Start practices maximize benefits for children and families with different characteristics under what types of circumstances?
   - How are gains sustained for children and families after the Head Start experience?

2. An overall research strategy rather than a single large-scale study is the appropriate framework for addressing critical Head Start research and evaluation questions.

   Three key approaches to guide this new strategy are: (a) implementation of an integrated and coordinated set of research and evaluation studies collectively designed to address the major questions; (b) use of diverse methodologies; (c) identification of "marker variables" for child functioning, family functioning, program characteristics, and community characteristics.

3. The diversity of Head Start children and families as well as the diversity of the communities in which they reside must be recognized explicitly in future evaluation and research.

4. Evaluation research must explicitly address diverse outcome indices related to children, families, communities, and institutions.

5. Multiple indicators and methods should be employed in the measurement of important outcomes.

6. Data collection procedures and techniques must be valid and appropriate for the particular research questions and the specific population.

7. Program variation must be explored while searching for explanations of differential outcomes.

8. Head Start research and evaluation studies can be greatly enhanced by building on the existing strengths of programs and program staffs.

The *Blueprint for the Future* panel recommended four research directions for inclusion in the overall strategy:

1. Longitudinal studies that seek to identify yearly and intermediate outcomes of a Head Start experience and that explore the interacting influences of preschool, family, and later schooling in mediating the long-term effects of child and family participation in Head Start.

2. Studies to identify quality ingredients in existing Head Start programs.

3. Studies of Head Start's emerging innovative program strategies.

4. Studies of special subpopulations of Head Start and other priority research and evaluation issues.

The *Blueprint for the Future* panel proposed four research support activities to create an environment which nurtures research and evaluation:

1. Establish an archive of significant Head Start data.

2. Develop a plan for Head Start measures identification and development.

3. Develop and implement a strategy for building Head Start's research and evaluation capacity.

4. Utilize information from existing Head Start administrative data bases for research and evaluation purposes.

In January 1992, a commissioner's advisory panel for implementing the *Blueprint for the Future* initially convened with the overall charge of devising steps that could be taken to realize the recommendations and objectives set forth in the *Blueprint*. This new panel consisted of ten members, five of whom served on the *Blueprint* panel, and five new members. One of the first tasks the panel assumed was identifying gaps in Head Start's knowledge base and proposing an integrated and coordinated set of research and evaluation studies collectively designed to address the major questions set forth in the *Blueprint*:

1. Which Head Start practices maximize benefits for children and families with different characteristics under what types of circumstances?

2. How are gains sustained for children and families after the Head Start experience?

The *Blueprint* implementation panel believed that research and evaluation efforts must address a wide range of outcome variables that reflect Head Start's multiple goals affecting children, families, and communities. After reviewing the existing Head Start research and considering the two major questions, the panel identified five research priority areas it considered needed the most immediate attention: bilingual/bicultural children and Head Start; health care and children with disabilities in Head Start; Head Start's influence on families: Head Start and the community; and the effect of the amount and intensity of participation in Head Start (or dose/response issues).

The *Blueprint* implementation panel proposed the establishment of a system of Head Start research centers. This set of regional centers would serve as "field stations" from which research on Head Start could better address the different populations now being served by Head Start programs and to explore ways of improving Head Start's effectiveness as a two-generation program. Also, such centers would provide stable organizations to support the longitudinal studies that are essential to study Head Start's long-term effect on children and families.

Also, the panel recommended that Head Start research move away from the use of nationally representative populations, which fail to represent in sufficient detail the considerable sociocultural and sociogeographic diversity in the Head Start populations. Instead, research efforts should focus on a number of carefully specified populations, in equally well-specified and circumscribed geographic areas, which in turn represent the spectrum of diversity in Head Start-eligible populations. Moreover, particularly in light of Head Start's tremendous expansion efforts, research needs to characterize all eligible children and families, rather than just those who participate or volunteer.

Finally, the panel considered it imperative that all research include explicit recognition of the diversity of the Head Start population. Research must address the differences and diversities of people—their competencies and strengths as well as their vulnerabilities. This recognition entails the use of specific cultural models customized to unique subpopulations, and measures sensitive to and normed for specific cultural groups.

CHAPTER 9

What's Ahead for Head Start
Conclusions and Recommendations

Over the past twenty-nine years, Head Start has an impressive record of achievement and has faced continual challenges. As we look ahead, the need for this comprehensive initiative is as salient as ever: poverty is escalating, family supports are weakening, and multiple challenges such as substance abuse and violence pose serious threats to both children and families.

What's ahead for Head Start?

As Head Start expands, there can be clear opportunities to ensure program quality and build on the innovative models and strategies which are the hallmarks of Head Start effectiveness.

It is important to recall again the broad social goal of Project Head Start. According to the Head Start performance standards:

> The overall goal of Head Start is to bring about a greater degree of social competence in the children of low-income families. By special competence is meant the child's everyday effectiveness in dealing with both the present environment and later responsibilities in school and life.

To accomplish this goal, it must be made clear that since the social context of society and family functioning affects child development and achievement; factors such as employment, health, substance abuse, and violence cannot be ignored if the child is to be supported. Thus, from the beginning, Head Start has attempted to balance two complementary but sometimes competing goals: providing a high-quality early childhood service including preschool education, health and social services, and parent support, and at the same time, attacking broader social issues. National policy and the accompanying fiscal support have unevenly supported both objectives, sometimes focusing narrowly on the quality of early childhood programs and at other times targeting resources at additional responsibilities such as family literacy.

At the local program level, grantees struggle to balance these dual commitments, particularly in view of the fact that the fiscal resources to accomplish both objectives have never been sufficient. As the challenges of poor communities have intensified and become even more complicated, grantees have found themselves in the uncomfortable position of having to trade off one set of commitments for another. An example of this trade-off is Omwake's concern that Head Start as an employment program for poor parents who have little education or training conflicts with Head Start as a quality preschool program with highly skilled teachers. Similarly, as will become increasingly evident with welfare reform legislation, the need for parent volunteers in Head Start classrooms conflicts with other equally legitimate goals for parents such as commitments to school, work, or family and community needs.

Clearly, as Head Start is re-examined and overhauled, specific attention must be given to an analysis of resource requirements outside of mandates simply to increase enrollment. There must be a better match between Head Start as an instrument for social change and the resources committed to do the job.

Given the limited funding for the broad mission of Head Start, there is an ongoing need to strengthen the coordination of services between Head Start grantees and other programs that provide literacy, education, training, and other self-sufficiency services. These programs include JOBS, Even Start, state and local education and training programs, and state family literacy programs. One way that such coordination could be achieved is by the direct provision of services offered by another program at the Head Start site, or off-site through contractual agreements.

The federal administrative agencies responsible for Head Start might better promote this type of coordination by providing direct technical assistance to Head Start grantees, disseminating information about grantees with successful coordination initiatives in place, and offering incentive grants or specific support related to fiscal questions.

What's ahead for Head Start?

We offer five priority areas for the future direction: Head Start for the twenty-first century should:

1. *Expand models of service delivery, with emphasis on serving infants and toddlers and offering full-day programs.*

   Head Start programs must be supported to provide expanded models of service. Parents have continuously highlighted the need for full-day care, a need underscored by welfare reform initiatives which emphasize the importance of employment for public assistance recipients.

   As Head Start programs expand in both size and types of programs, special attention must be given to organizational development issues, i.e., maintaining the "family feeling" and inclusive culture that have been the hallmarks of success.

2. *Showcase excellent programs.*

   Head Start must do a better job of disseminating its promising practices and innovations to audiences within Head Start, within the larger early childhood and human services fields, and to the public at large. Public relations, marketing, and communication plans have been notably absent during the past twenty-nine years. Rather, most publicity about Head Start has been reactive to research or legislative challenges. A proactive strategy to share the lessons and successes of Head Start programs is needed.

3. *Address the difficult questions about child and family outcomes.*

   Outcome measures are an issue that has been skirted for a long time. Head Start must actively address this issue and devise its own measures of quality. The work of the *Blueprint* panel is significant and should be implemented.

4. *Strengthen the management and administrative capacity.*

As has been indicated, clear job requirements and management training for Head Start directors and coordinators for education, social services, and other roles have been virtually nonexistent. Given the pressures of expansion and the aging infrastructures of Head Start facilities and transportation systems, the importance of strengthening administrative capacity is evident. Management training and leadership development will also be helpful as Head Start staff devise coordination strategies between an array of local, state, and federal initiatives for children. Further, this leadership is crucial if Head Start programs, as a whole, intend to tackle difficult questions of curriculum and family needs.

5. *Continue to be creative in the face of complex choices.*

Head Start has masterfully balanced the dilemmas and trade-offs that have been part of its social history since 1965. These dilemmas and choices are multiple and complex. How can Head Start achieve full funding to support every child while also seeking the funds for each child to have the option of multiple years of services? How can standards of excellence be strengthened or maintained while preserving the flexibility of local programs? How can increasingly larger numbers of children and families be served while continuing to value the strong personal nature of staff-family interactions?

Head Start programs have successfully negotiated these dilemmas in the past and will continue to need a high level of creativity to address these and other issues in the future.

What's ahead for Head Start? In summary, an emphasis on:

- growth
- quality
- assessment and strengthening

As this book is being completed, for example, two major events affecting Head Start are evident:

- First, final appropriations for FY 1994 included expansion of Head Start to $3.3 billion (up from $2.8 billion), while nearly all other early childhood-related programs received funding at the same level as last year.

- Second, the Secretary of Health and Human Services has completed a major review of Head Start. By convening an advisory committee on Head Start quality and expansion in July 1993, the federal government launched an in-depth study on the Head Start program for the purpose of developing recommendations to improve and strengthen the program in a time of expansion. The deliberations of that group emphasize serving younger children and strengthening program quality in a variety of ways.

All signs indicate that Head Start will thrive, yet face challenges, as it moves toward the twenty-first century. Yet it is important to bear in mind that Head Start, no matter how comprehensive or well administered, can only do so much to combat poor prenatal care, inadequate nutrition, poor neighborhoods, and the racial and gender discrimination that touch the lives of many Head Start families. Head Start is not a panacea for poverty, and attempts to posture it as such will lead to an inevitable fall. Clearly, it will be unwise to strengthen our national investment in Project Head Start if this investment is not accompanied by the continuation, improvement, and expansion of other services and institutions that affect Head Start children and families.

References

Abt Associates. Home Start Evaluation Study–Interim Reports 5 and 6. Cambridge, MA: Abt Associates, 1974 and 1975. (EDI07380)

Adams, G., and K. Pittman. *Adolescent and Young Adult Fathers: Problems and Solutions.* Washington, DC: Children's Defense Fund, 1988.

Advisory Committee on Head Start Quality and Expansion. *Creating a Twenty-first Century Head Start.* Washington, DC: HHS, 1993.

Andrews, Susan Ring, Janet Berstein Blumenthal, Dale L. Johnson, Alfred J. Kahn, Carol J. Ferguson, Thomas M., Lasater, Paul E. Malone, and Doris B. Wallace. "The Skills of Mothering: A Study of Parent-Child Development Centers." *Monograph of the Society for Research in Child Development* 47 (6 Serial No. 198) (1982).

Reports the results of the PCDC experiment from 1970 to 1975 in Birmingham, Houston, and New Orleans. Significant differences were found between program and control groups in maternal behavior and Stanford-Binet scores. The limitations and strengths of the projects are discussed in the framework of program goals. Implications for parent education, future research, and social policy are examined.

Applied Management Sciences. *Evaluation of the Process of Mainstreaming Handicapped Children into Project Head Start, Phase I Executive Summary.* Silver Spring, MD, April 28, 1978A (Contract No. HEW 105-76-113).

Applied Management Sciences. *Evaluation of the Process of Mainstreaming Handicapped Children into Project Head Start, Phase H Executive Summary.* Silver Spring, MD, December 15, 1978B (Contract No. HEW 105-76-113).

Arenas, S. Innovation in Bilingual/Multicultural Curriculum Development. *Children Today* 9 (1980): 17–21.

Austin, Bobby W. *What a Piece of Work Is Man.* Battle Creek, MI: W.K. Kellogg Foundation, 1992.

Barclay, Lisa K. "Using Spanish as the Language of Instruction with Mexican American Head Start Children: A Reevaluation Using Meta-analysis." *Perceptual and Motor Skills* 56 (1983): 359–366.

Found that the use of Spanish as the language of instruction resulted in larger effect sizes than did the use of English, both languages, or a control treatment using arts, crafts, and music activities. Doubts about the efficacy of beginning instruction in non-English speakers' native languages are questioned.

Barnett, W.S. "Benefits of Compensatory Preschool Education." *Journal of Human Resources* 27 (1992): 279–312.

Barnett, W.S., and C.M. Escobar. "Economic Costs and Benefits of Early Intervention." In S.J. Meisels and J.P. Shonkoff, eds., *Handbook of Early Childhood Intervention.* New York: Cambridge University Press, 1990, pp. 560–582.

Introduces the methods and findings of economic research on early intervention and explores the implications of those findings for research, policy, and practice.

Barnow, B.S. "The Effects of Head Start and Socioeconomic Status on Cognitive Development of Disadvantaged Children." Ph.D. dissertation, University of Wisconsin, 1973.

Reviews the controversy surrounding the Westinghouse report, particularly the statistical problems involved in Head Start evaluations, and reanalyzes the data using individual, rather than grouped, data. Barnow's reanalysis also includes more socioeconomic and demographic variables than does the Westinghouse study.

Barret, Robert L., and Bryan E. Robinson. "A Descriptive Study of Teenage Expectant Fathers." *Family Relations* 31 (1982A): 349–352.

Reports demographic data on a sample of twenty-six adolescent expectant fathers and their relationships with the expectant mothers and their families. The study finds that the fathers maintained positive relationships with the expectant mother's families and wanted to participate with the children.

Barret, Robert L., and Bryan E. Robinson. "Teenage Fathers: Neglected Too Long." *Social Work* 27 (November 1982B): 484–488.

Reviews the literature on adolescent fathers and offers recommendations for improving services to unwed adolescent parents.

Beatty, L. *Involvement of Black Fathers in Head Start.* Paper presented at the annual meeting of the American Educational Research Association, San Francisco, 1989.

Becher, R. *Parent Involvement: A Review of Research and Principles of Successful Practice.* Washington, DC: National Institute of Education, 1984.

Becker, W.C. "Project Head Start: A Legacy of the War on Poverty." *Merrill Palmer Quarterly* (1981).

Berrueta-Clement, J.R., L.J. Schweinhart, W.S. Barnett, A.S. Epstein, and D.P. Weikart. *Changed Lives—The Effects of the Perry Preschool Program on Youths Through Age Nineteen.* Ypsilanti, MI: High/Scope Educational Research Foundation, 1984.

Reports the results of a longitudinal study that sought to demonstrate whether or not preschool education of high quality could alter the lives of children living in poverty. The study demonstrated that high quality preschool intervention can prevent developmental attrition and can make a positive impact on the future lives of its participants.

Besharov, D.J. "New Directions for Head Start." *The World and I* (January 1992A): 515–531.

Reviews Head Start initiatives designed to address problems of the family including parent-child centers, child and family resource programs, comprehensive child development centers, family service centers, and family support programs.

Besharov, D.J. "Why Head Start Needs a Re-Start: Poverty, Violence Threaten the Gains." *The Washington Post* (February 2, 1992B): C-1, C-4.

Reviews rationale for shift in emphasis of Head Start to include a greater focus on securing both the child and the family.

Besharov, D.J. "Fresh Start." *The New Republic* (June 14, 1993): 14–16.

Besharov, D.J., and T.W. Hartle. "Head Start: Making a Popular Program Work." *Pediatrics* 79 (1987): 440–441.

Billingsley, Andrew. *Climbing Jacob's Ladder: The Enduring Legacy of African-American Families.* New York: Simon and Schuster, 1992.

Bloom, Benjamin. *Stability and Change in Human Characteristics.* New York: Wiley and Sons, 1964.

Bollinger, Linda K. "Superstar." *Reporter* (1981): 13–15.

Calls Head Start a superstar of social programs because of its popularity and success. Highlights of Head Start's history are presented.

Braucht, G.N., D. Brakarsh, D. Follingstad, and K.L. Berry. "Deviant Drug Use in Adolescents: A Review of Psychosocial Correlates." *Psychological Bulletin* 70 (1973): 92–106.

Bronfenbrenner, Urie. "Is Early Intervention Effective?" In M. Guttentag and E. Struning, eds., *Handbook of Evaluation*

Research, Vol. 2. Newbury Park, CA: Sage Publications, 1975, pp. 519–604.

Bronfenbrenner, Urie. *The Ecology of Human Development.* Cambridge, MA: Harvard University Press, 1979A.

Bronfenbrenner, Urie. "Head Start, a Retrospective View: The Founders." In Edward Zigler and Jeanette Valentine, eds., *Project Head Start.* New York: Free Press, 1979B, pp. 77–88.

Brush, L., Gaidurgis, A. and C. Best. *Indices of Head Start Program Quality.* Washington, DC: ACYF, 1993.

Caliguri, J. "Will Parents Take Over Head Start Programs?" *Urban Education* 5 (1970): 54.

Campbell, Donald T., and Albert Erlebacher. "How Regression Artifacts in Quasi-Experimental Evaluation Can Mistakenly Make Compensatory Education Look Harmful." In Jerome Hellmuch, ed., *Disadvantaged Child Volume III: Compensatory Education: A National Debate.* New York: Brunner/Mazel, 1970A, pp. 185–210.

Critiques matching and analysis of covariance and partial correlation; they produce regression artifacts that make compensatory programs look deleterious. Other inadequacies of social science methodology, such as that used in the Westinghouse report, are cited. Randomization experiments are suggested as a better alternative.

Campbell, Donald T., and Albert Erlebacher. "Reply to the Replies." In Jerome Hellmuch, ed., *Disadvantaged Child Volume III: Compensatory Education: A National Debate.* New York: Brunner/Mazel, 1970B, pp. 221–225.

Point-by-point comments are made in this reply to Cicirelli, Evans, and Schiller in the debate on the the bias of the Westinghouse report. While Cicirelli, Evans, and Schiller argue that the magnitude of bias was minimal, Campbell and Erlebacher emphasize their opinion that the degree is unascertainable for two reasons: First, the lack of information on the characteristics of the populations from which matches were chosen prior to matching; second, lack of information on the factorial composition of the covariates.

Carter, J. "A Statement in New Hampshire." *The Presidential Campaign, 1976, Vol. 1* Washington, DC: U.S. Government Printing Office, 1978.

Carter, S. and U.J. Oyemade. *Parents Getting a Head Start Against Drugs: A Primary Prevention Curriculum.* Rockville, MD: HHS/OSAP, 1990.

A substance abuse prevention curriculum for Head Start parents. It is guided by research that identifies factors that place some families at higher risk of substance abuse and characteristics that make drug abuse less likely. Curriculum content focuses on drug information, self-esteem, communication, stress, drugs in the community, health issues, values and peer pressure, family management and relations, and developing support networks. A discussion/experiential approach guides activities that build on the family's culture and enables families to incorporate practices in their lives.

Cazenave, N.A. "Middle-Income Black Fathers: An Analysis of the Provider Role." *The Family Coordinator* 27 (1979): 583–593.

Chafel, J.A. "Funding Head Start: What Are the Issues?" *American Journal of Orthopsychiatry* 62 (1992): 9–21.

Examines issues regarding the improvement of services relative to funding. Presents an analysis of competing policy options and makes recommendations for future funding.

Charters, B. and L. Garey. "A New Kind of Head Start on Science." *NHSA Journal* (Winter 1992): 61.

Chavkin, David, and Peggy Pizzo, "Head Start and Medicaid: A New Marriage for the 1990s." *NHSA* (Spring 1991): 53–57.

Children's Defense Fund. "A Children's Defense Budget: An Analysis of the President's FY 1984 Budget and Children Reports." Washington, DC: CDF, 1983A.

Children's Defense Fund. "Give More Children a Head Start. It Pays." Washington, DC: CDF, 1983B.

Provides a brief overview of Head Start's history, benefits, and accomplishments. Enrollments and appropriations are presented from 1965 through 1983. Six Head Start programs are examined to show what a difference the program means for individuals from diverse backgrounds in diverse settings.

Children's Defense Fund. *A Children's Defense Budget: An Analysis of the President's FY 1985 Budget and Children.* Washington, DC: CDF, 1984.

Fourth annual analysis of the president's budget and its effects on a variety of children's programs in the areas of child care, education, maternal and child health, child welfare, child nutrition, AFDC, youth employment, and others.

Children's Defense Fund. *Black and White Children in America: Key Facts.* Washington, DC: CDF, 1985.

Provides overall and comparative data on the status of black and white children in the United States in several areas: child welfare; adolescent pregnancy; income and poverty; employment and unemployment: maternal employment and child care; and child health and education.

Children's Defense Fund. "The State of America's Children." Washington, DC: CDF, 1991.

Children's Defense Fund. "Congress Improves Head Start." Washington, DC: CDF, October 1992.

Children's Defense Fund. "Head Start Moves into the 1990s." Washington, DC: CDF, March 1993A.

Children's Defense Fund. "Statement on the Quality and Benefits of Head Start." Washington, DC: CDF, March 5, 1993B.

Supports President Clinton's plan to expand Head Start; states that there are many excellent programs; states that, as could be expected with a program serving more than 700,000 children through nearly 1,400 grantees, some Head Start programs need improvement. Nevertheless, the fact that some programs need improvement should not be used as an excuse to oppose full funding for Head Start.

Clinton, Bill. Budget Proposal for Fiscal Year 1994. Released April 9, 1993.

Cole, O. Jackson, and Valora Washington. "A Critical Analysis of the Effects of Head Start on Minority Children." *Journal of Negro Education* 55 (1986): 91–106.

Critiques Head Start research with emphasis on determining its effects on minority children. Urges more involvement by minority scholars in Head Start research.

Collins, R.C. *Head Start Salaries: 1989–90 Staff Salary Survey.* Alexandria, VA: NHSA, 1990.

Collins, R.C. "Head Start: Steps Toward a Two-Generation Program Strategy." *Young Children* 48 (1993): 25–33, 72–73.

Collins, R.C., and P.R. Anderson. *Head Start Substance Abuse Guide.* Washington, DC: HHS, 1991. (Publication. No. [ACF] 91–31265)

Outlines issues which Head Start grantees need to address and suggests resources and strategies consistent with Head Start's mission to respond to these issues.

Collins, R.C., and Dennis Deloria. "Head Start Research: A New Chapter." *Children Today* 12 (July–August 1983): 15–19.

Discusses the Head Start Synthesis, Evaluation, and Utilization Project conducted by CSR, Inc., which involves a review of Head Start literature from 1965 to the present. Findings of the study reveal: Head Start produces substantial gains in children's cognitive and language development; Head Start has grown more effective over the years; and the most needy children appear to benefit from the program. It was also found that Head Start favorably affected social development, task orientation, curiosity, and socialization of handicapped children. The positive effects of Head Start on children's health, families, and the community are also discussed.

Collins, R.C., and P. Kinney. *Head Start Research and Evaluation: Background and Overview.* Vienna, VA: Collins Management Consulting, Inc., 1993.

Committee for Economic Development. *Children in Need! Investment Strategies for the Educationally Disadvantaged.* Washington, DC: Committee for Economic Development, 1987.

Addresses the needs of children at risk of failure, whose problems are largely being bypassed by local state and local education reforms. Outlines three-part strategy for breaking the cycle of failure that includes early intervention, restructuring of the schools, and programs targeted to adolescents at risk of dropping out and those who have already left the system.

Committee for Economic Development. *The Unfinished Agenda: A New Vision for Child Development.* Washington, DC: Committee for Economic Development, 1991.

Analyzes the results of the education reform movement and finds that most state and local initiatives have been piecemeal, conflicting, and have lacked a true understanding of the complex needs that affect children's ability to learn. Urges the nation to develop a coordinated and comprehensive strategy or investment including strengthening families.

Congressional Research Service. *Head Start Program: Background Information and Issues.* Washington, DC: Author, 1990.

Reports that only 6 percent of Head Start programs use Head Start funds to provide full-day services that run nine hours or more.

Cook, Paddy S., R.C. Petersen, and D.T. Moore. *Alcohol, Tobacco, and Other Drugs May Harm the Unborn.* Rockville, MD: HHS/OSAP, 1990. (HHS Publication No. ADM 90–1711)

Summarizes the research related to the effects of alcohol, tobacco, and other drugs on the fetus and the newborn.

Copple, C. M. Cline, and A. Smith. *Paths to the Future: Long-Term Effects of Head Start in the Philadelphia School District.* Washington, DC: HHS, 1987.

Coulson, J.M. et al. "Effects of Different Head Start Program Approaches on Children of Different Characteristics: Report on Analyses of Data from 1966–67 and 1967–68 National Evaluations." Technical Memorandum TM-48620001/00. Santa Monica, CA: Systems Development Corp., August 19, 1972. (ER/C #ED 0720859)

Council for Early Childhood Professional Recognition. *CDA Competence Newsletter.* Washington, DC: Author, July 1993.

Craig, S. "The Educational Needs of Children Living with Violence." *Phi Delta Kappan* (September 1992): 67–71.

CSR, Inc. Refer to McKey et al.

Datta, Lois-ellin. "Another Spring and Other Hopes: Some Findings from National Evaluations of Project Head Start." In Edward Zigler and Jeanette Valentine, eds., *Project Head Start.* New York: The Free Press, 1979, pp. 405–432.

Delgade, Melvin. "Hispanic Adolescence and Substance Abuse: Implications for Research, Treatment, and Prevention." In A. Shiffman and K.E. Davis, eds., *Ethnic Issues in Adolescent Mental Health.* Newbury Park, CA: Sage Publications, 1990.

Presents a demographic profile of Hispanics. Reviews literature on Hispanic adolescent substance abuse. Suggests research, treatment, and prevention strategies for addressing substance abuse in Hispanic communities.

Department of Health and Human Services. *Head Start Expansion: Grantee Experiences.* Washington, DC: Author, May 1993.

Dinkmeyer, D. *Systematic Training for Effective Parenting.* Circle Pines, MN: American Guidance Service, 1980.

Dittmann, L. "Project Head Start Becomes a Long Distance Runner." *Young Children* 35 (6) (September 1980): 2–9.

Dunteman, G. et al. *A Report on Two National Samples of Head Start Classes: Some Aspects of Child Development of Participants in Full Year 1967–1968 and 1968–1969 Programs.* Research Triangle Park, NC: Research Triangle Institute, July 1972.

Dupont, Robert L. *Stopping Alcohol and Other Drug Use Before It Starts: The Future of Prevention.* Rockville, MD: HHS/OSAP, 1989.

Outlines the nature of the alcoholic and other drug problems in the U.S. and the current state of knowledge about how to prevent AOD problems. Also analyzes available prevention programs and discribes the next steps in the nation's efforts to prevent AOD use by youth.

Edwards, E. Daniel and Margie Egbert-Edwards. "American Indian Adolescents Combating Problems of Substance Use and Abuse through a Community Model." In A. Stiffman and L.E. Davis, eds., *Ethnic Issues in Adolescent Mental Health.* Newbury Park, CA: Sage Publications, 1990.

Presents data on the incidence of substance abuse in the American Indian community. Identifies problems contributing to substance use in Indian communities. Suggests strategies for treating and preventing substance abuse in American Indian cultures.

Ellsworth Associates. *The Commissioner's Panel on Head Start Research and Evaluation Activities: Implementing the Blueprint. Research Priorities to Implement the Blueprint.* Washington, DC: HHS, March 1993.

In 1990, an advisory panel for the Head Start Evaluation Design Project recommended an overall strategy and a set of guiding principles for future Head Start research and evaluation efforts which are detailed in the report, *Head Start Research and Evaluation: A Blueprint for the Future.* In January 1992, the Commissioner's Panel for Implementing the Blueprint convened to devise steps that could be taken to realize the recommendations of the *Blueprint.* The panel identified six research priority areas: bilingual/bicultural children and Head Start, health care, children with disabilities, the influence on the family, community impact, and the effect of amount and intensity of participation in Head Start.

Farran, D.C., B. Silveri, and A. Culp. "Public School Preschools and the Disadvantaged." *New Directions for Child Development* 53 (1991): 65–73.

Gaines, R. *Helping Handicapped Children: Recommendations for Model Programs in Head Start Centers.* Los Angeles: University of California, 1979.

Identifies the handicapping condition, diagnostic assessment, social and cognitive intervention, special services for the handicapping condition, and parent involvement.

Gamble, Thomas J., and Edward Zigler. "The Head Start Synthesis Project: A Critique." *Developmental Psychology* 10 (1989): 267–274.

Identifies flaws in studies of the effects of Head Start published in McKey et al. *The Impact of Head Start on Children, Families, and Communities: Head Start Synthesis Project* (1985).

Garbarino, J., N. Dubrow, K. Kostelny, and C. Pardo. *Children in Danger: Coping with the Effects of Community Violence.* San Francisco: Jossey-Bass, 1992.

Argues that the escalating rate of violence in U.S. cities means that large numbers of children are growing up in conditions that have been described as "war zones." Experts describe the impact of violence on many children as post-traumatic stress disorder. Moreover, the younger the child, the greater the threat of exposure to violence to healthy development. Children who experienced an initial trauma before the age of eleven were three times more likely to develop psychiatric symptoms than those who experienced their first traumas as teens. Chronic exposure to violence can have serious developmental consequences for children including psychological disorders, grief and loss reactions, impaired intellectual development and school problems, truncated moral development, pathological adaptation to violence, and identification with the aggressor. Still, most children are able to cope with dangerous environments and maintain resilience as long as their parents are not stressed beyond their capacity to cope.

Gary, L.D., ed. *Black Men.* Beverly Hills, CA: Sage Publications, 1981.

General Accounting Office. *Early Childhood and Family Development Programs Improve the Quality of Life for Low-Income Families.* Washington, DC: GAO, 1979. (Report #HRD-79-40)

General Accounting Office. *Poor Preschool-Aged Children Numbers Increase but Most Not in Preschool.* Washington, DC: General Accounting Office, July 1993. (GAO/HRD-93-111BR)

Reports to the chairman, Subcommittee on Children, Family, Drugs, and Alcoholism, Committee on Labor and Human Resources, U.S. Senate. The report finds that from 1980 to 1990, the number of poor preschool-aged children increased 28 percent compared with an increase among all preschool-aged children of only 16 percent. One-third of poor preschool-aged children participated in preschool, compared with more than 60 percent of the highest income three-and four-year-olds.

Goodman, I., and J. Brady. *The Challenge of Coordination.* Newton, MA: Education Development Center, 1988.

Gordon, E.W. "Parent and Child Centers: Their Basis in the Behavioral and Educational Sciences—An Invited Critique." *American Journal of Orthopsychiatry* 41 (1) (1971): 39–42.

Gordon, E.W. "Evaluation During the Early Years of Head Start." In E. Zigler and J. Valentine, eds., *Project Head Start.* New York: Free Press, 1979, pp. 399–404.

Reviews the early period in the development of Head Start research and evaluation. Identifies four major issues and experiences: 1) a tension between the use of small-scale controlled experiments on a large-scale field experiment and the employment of other techniques to collect and analyze mass data; 2) the hurried development of measuring instruments; 3) the development of the Head Start research and evaluation centers; and 4) the emergence of an anti-evaluation and anti-testing sentiment.

Gore, Al. *Creating a Government That Works Better and Costs Less: Report of the National Performance Review.* Washington, DC: GPO, 1993.

Gray, S., and R. Klaus. "An Experimental Preschool Program for Culturally Deprived Children." *Child Development* 36 (1965): 887–898.

Greenberg, Polly. *The Devil Has Slippery Shoes: A Biased Biography of the Child Development Group of Mississippi.* Washington, DC: Youth Policy Institute, 1990, p. 3.

Greenberg, Polly. "Head Start—Part of a Multi-Pronged Anti-Poverty Effort for Children and Their Families . . . Before the Beginning: A Participant's View." *Young Children* 45 (6) (September 1990).

History of Head Start's formation and summarization of activities during its conceptualization. Part of twenty-fifth anniversary celebration.

Grotberg, Edith H. *Review of Research 1965 to 1969.* Washington, DC: OEO, 1969.

Reviews research and demonstration projects supported by OEO's Research and Evaluation Office.

Hale, B.A., V. Seitz, and E. Zigler. "Health Services and Head Start: A Forgotten Formula." *Journal of Applied Developmental Psychology* 11 (1990): 447–458.

Hall, D.M. "Child Health Promotion, Screening, and Surveillance." *Journal of Child Psychology and Psychiatry* 33 (1992): 649–658.

Harmon, C., and E. Hanley. "Administrative Aspects of Head Start." In Edward Zigler and J. Valentine, eds., *Project Head Start.* New York: Free Press, 1979, pp. 379–398.

Harrington, Michael. *The Other America: Poverty in the United States.* New York: Macmillan, 1962.

Hawkins, David J. et al. *Preparing for the Drug (Free) Years: A Family Activity Book.* Seattle, WA: Comprehensive Health Education Foundation, 1987.

Summary of activities for families for prevention of substance abuse.

Hawkins, J.D., D. Lesliner, and R.F. Catalano. "Childhood Predictors and the Prevention of Adolescent Substance Abuse." *NIDA Research Monograph 56, Etiology of Drug Abuse—Implications for Prevention* (1985): 75–126.

Hebbler, K. "An Old and a New Question on the Effects of Early Education for Children from Low-Income Families." *Educational Evaluation and Policy Analysis* 7 (3) (1985): 207–216.

Compared Head Start registrants who did and did not attend Head Start in three different cohorts in Maryland and found that maternal education and family income were lower for attendees than for non-attendees.

Hill, Charles H. "Head Start: A Problem of Assumptions." *Education* 92 (1972): 89–93.

Hill, Martha S., and Michael Ponza. "Poverty and Welfare Dependence Across Generations." *Economic Outlook USA* (Summer 1983): 61–64.

Holden, Constance. "Head Start Enters Adulthood." *News and Comment* 247 (1990):1400–1402.

Author suggests that after twenty-five years we don't know much about how early childhood intervention programs work, but current research suggests they should be extended beyond early childhood.

Hood, J. "Caveat Emptor: The Head Start Scam." *Policy Analysis,* #187 (December 1992). Washington, DC: Cato Institute.

Hood, J. "What's Wrong with Head Start?" *Wall Street Journal* (February 19, 1993): A14.

Horn, W.F. *Administration on Children, Youth, and Families. Accomplishments: FY 1989 to FY 1993.* Washington, DC: ACYF, 1993.

Huey, John. "How We Can Win the War on Poverty." *Fortune* (April 10, 1989): 125–128, 130, 132, 134, 136.

Hunt, J. McVicker. *Intelligence and Experience.* New York: Ronald Press, 1961.

Hunt, J. McVicker. "Parent and Child Centers: Their Basis in the Behavioral and Educational Sciences." *American Journal of Orthopsychiatry* 41 (1) (1971): 13–38.

Johnson, Richard H. *Letter of Transmittal to the Office of the Commissioner from the National Parent Involvement Task Force.* Washington, DC: HHS/OHDS/ACYF, March 11, 1986.

Johnston, L.D., P.M. O'Malley, and J.G. Bachman. *Drug Abuse Among American High School Students, College Students, and Other Young Adults: National Trends Through 1987.* Washington, DC: National Institute of Drug Abuse, 1988, pp. 13–22.

Kagan, S.L., and E. Zigler, eds. *Early Schooling: The National Debate.* New Haven, CT: Yale University Press, 1987.

Kandel, D., R.C. Kessler, and R.S. Margulies. "Adolescent Interaction into Stages of Drug Use: A Developmental Analysis." In D. Kandel, ed., *Longitudinal Research on Drug Use: Empirical Findings and Methodological Issues.* Washington, DC: Hemisphere-Wiley, 1978A.

Kandel, D., R.C. Kessler, and R.S. Margulies. "Antecedents of Imitation into Stages of Drug Use: A Developmental Analysis." *Journal of Youth and Adolescence* 7 (1978B): 13–40.

Kennedy, E. "Head Start in the Right Direction." *Washington Post* (February 15, 1992).

Kennedy, E.M. "The Head Start Transition Project: Head Start Goes to Elementary School." In E. Zigler and S.J. Styfco, eds., *Head Start and Beyond: A National Plan for Extended*

Childhood Intervention. New Haven, CT: Yale University Press, 1993.

Kirschner Associates. *A National Survey of the Impacts of Head Start Centers on Community Institutions.* Albuquerque, NM: Kirschner Associates, May 1970.

Knitzer, J. "Parental Involvement: The Elixir of Change."In Dennis N. McFadden, ed., *Early Childhood Development Programs and Services: Planning for Action.* Washington, DC: National Association for the Education of Young Children, 1972, pp. 83–95.

Kotelchuck, M., and J.B. Richmond. "Head Start: Evolution of a Successful Comprehensive Child Development Program." *Pediatrics* 79 (1987): 441–445.

Authors take issue with the criticism of Head Start by Besharov and Hartle (1987). They suggest that the focus only on cognitive gains is misguided in light of the Head Start mission. They conclude that there can never be a single "definitive" evaluation of the comprehensive Head Start program.

Kozel, N.J. and E.A. Adams. "Epidemiology of Drug Abuse: An Overview." *Science* 234 (1986): 970–974.

Krohn, M., J. Massey, R. Laner, and W. Skinner. "Social Bonding Theory and Adolescent Cigarette Smoking: A Longitudinal Analysis." *Journal of Health and Social Behavior* 24 (1983): 337–349.

Kunjufo, Jawanza. *Developing Positive Self-Images and Discipline in Black Children.* Chicago: African-American Images, 1984.

Presents a review of the literature related to self-concept in African Americans. Specific strategies for enhancing self-esteem in African American children are presented.

Lally, J.R., P.L. Mangione, and A.S. Honig. *Syracuse University Family Development Research Program: Long-Range Impact of an Early Intervention with Low-Income Children and Their Families.* San Francisco: Center for Child and Family Studies, Far West Laboratory for Educational Research and Development, 1987.

Lally, J.R., P.L. Mangione, A.S. Honig, and D.S. Wittmer. "More Pride, Less Delinquency: Findings From the Ten-Year Follow-up Study of the Syracuse University Family Development Research Program." *Zero to Three* 8 (4) (May 1988): 13–18.

Lamb, M.E., and A. Sagi, eds. *Fatherhood and Family Policy.* Hillsdale, NJ: Lawrence Erlbaum Associates, 1983.

Laosa, Luis. "Social Policies Toward Children of Diverse Ethnic, Racial, and Language Groups in the United States." In H.W. Stevenson and A.E. Siegel, eds., *Child Development and Social Policy.* Chicago: University of Chicago Press, 1985, pp. 1–109.

Traces major trends in the evolution of social policies toward children that bear directly on issues of ethnic, racial, and language diversity. Also examines the public attitudes, intellectual assumptions, and sociodemographic trends that have accompanied these policy developments. The impact of social scientists on these policies is also explored.

Larsen, L.E. "The Influence of Parents and Peers During Adolescence: The Situation Hypothesis Revisited." *Journal of Marriage and Family* 34 (1972): 67–74.

Larsen, L.E. "An Examination of the Salience Hierarchy During Adolescence: The Influence of the Family." *Adolescence* 9 (1974): 317–332.

Lawrence, T.S., and J.D. Vellerman. "Correlates of Student Drug Use in Suburban High School." *Psychiatry* 35 (1974): 129–136.

Layzer, J.I., B.D. Goodson, and M. Moss. *Life in Preschool.* Washington, DC: U.S. Dept. of Education Office of Policy and Planning, 1993.

Lee, V.E., J. Brooks-Gunn, E. Schnur, and F.R. Liaw. "Are Head Start Effects Sustained? A Longitudinal Follow-Up Comparison of Disadvantaged Children Attending Head Start, No Preschool, and Other Preschool Programs." *Child Development* 61 (1990): 495–507.

Studies the prolonged effects (into kindergarten and grade 1) of Project Head Start on disadvantaged African American children. Findings suggest that children who attended Head Start maintained educationally substantive gains in general cognitive/analytic ability, especially when compared to children without preschool experience.

Lee, V.E., E. Schnur and J. Brooks-Gunn "Does Head Start Work? A One Year Follow-Up Comparison of Disadvantaged Children Attending Head Start, No Preschool, and Other Preschool Programs." *Developmental Psychology* 24 (2) (1988): 210–222.

Examines the success of Head Start as a preschool program for economically disadvantaged children. Reports that Head Start "proved an impressive instrument of short-term change, even compared with other preschool experience."

Leik, Robert K., Mary Anne Chalkley, and Nancy Peterson. "Policy Implictions of Involving Parents in Head Start." In E. Anderson and R. Hula, eds., *The Reconstruction of Family Policy*. Westport, CT: Greenwood Press, forthcoming.

Lewis, T. Internal ACYF memo to Elizabeth Ussery, associate commissioner, Head Start Bureau, December 9, 1988.

Maddox, G.L., ed. *The Domesticated Drug: Drinking among Collegians*. New Haven, CT: College and University Press, 1970.

Mallory, Nancy J., and Nancy A. Goldsmith. "Head Start Works: Two Head Start Veterans Share Their Views." *Young Children* 45 (6) (1990): 36–39.

Evaluates Head Start in terms of comprehensive services, parent involvement, and family support, commitment to meeting local needs, training and technical assistance support, and collaborative approach.

Mann, A.J., A. Harrell, and M. Hurt. *A Review of Head Start Research Since 1969 and an Annotated Bibliography*.

Washington, DC: HEW, 1977. (DHEW Publication No. 78–31102)

> Reviews Head Start research and provides an annotated bibliography of literature relating to the Head Start program. Briefly summarized are the findings and extent of research related to the impact of Head Start in the following five areas: child health, social development of the child, cognitive development of the child, the family, and the community.

McAdoo, J.L. "Black Father and Child Interactions." In L.E. Gary, ed., *Black Men*. Newbury Park, CA: Sage Publications, 1981, pp. 115–130.

McBride, D. *Parental and Peer Influences on Adolescent Drug Use.* Rockville, MD: National Institute on Drug Abuse, 1978.

McKey, R.H., I. Condelli, H. Ganson, B. Barrett, C. McConkey, and M. Plantz. *The Impact of Head Start on Children, Families, and Communities.* Washington, DC: CSR, Inc., June 1985.

Meisels, S.J. "Developmental Screening in Early Childhood: The Interaction of Research and Social Policy." In L. Breslow, J.E. Fielding, and L.B. Lave, eds., *Annual Review of Public Health, Vol. 9.* Palo Alto, CA: Annual Review, 1988, pp. 522–550.

Midco Educational Associates, Inc. *Investigation of the Effects of Parent Participation in Head Start* (Non-Technical Report). Washington, DC: HHS/ACYF, 1972A.

Midco Educational Associates, Inc. *Perspectives on Parent Participation in Project Head Start: An Analysis and Critique.* Denver, CO: Midco, 1972B.

> Describes a project which investigated the impact of Head Start parent participation on the program's quality, on institutional changes in the community, on the Head Start children, and on the Head Start parents themselves. Two types of parent participation were investigated: 1) parents in decision-making roles, and 2) parents in learner roles. Another type of involvement in

which parents were paid employees in Head Start programs was also studied.

Miller, Jones Dalton. "The Study of African American Children's Development Contributions to Reformulation Development Paradigms." In Diana T. Slaughter, ed., *Black Children and Poverty: A Developmental Perspective.* San Francisco: Jossey Bass, 1988.

Mitchell, A., M. Seligson and F. Marx. *Early Childhood Programs and the Public Schools.* Dover, MA: Auburn House, 1989.

Moynihan, Daniel P. *Family and Nation.* New York: Harcourt Brace Jovanovich, 1986.

Looks at the disintegration of the American family. Argues that when the family suffers, the young suffer most.

Muenchow, Susan, and Susan Shays. *Head Start in the 1980s. Review and Recommendations. A Report Requested by the President of the United States.* Washington, DC: HHS/OHDS/ACYF, Head Start Bureau, September 1980.

A fifteenth-anniversary report on Project Head Start. The report is divided into five sections: an inventory of Head Start programs and demonstration projects, a review of the success of Head Start programs, a presentation of problems in Head Start programs, a presentation of policy options for the 1980s, and a list of recommendations.

Myers, B.J., H.C. Olson, and K. Kallenbach. "Cocaine-Exposed Infants: Myths and Misunderstandings." *Zero to Three,* 13 (1) (1992): 1–5.

National Association for Perinatal Addiction Research and Education. Background file. Chicago: 1989.

National Association for Perinatal Addiction Research and Education. "Strategies for Teaching Young Children Prenatally Exposed to Drugs." *NAPARE UPDATE* (March 1991).

National Association for the Education of Young Children. *Statement on Head Start Expansion.* Washington, DC: NAEYC, March 31, 1993.

National Center for Children in Poverty. *Five Million Children: 1993 Update.* New York: National Center for Children in Poverty, 1993.

National Commission on Children. *Beyond Rhetoric: A New Agenda for Children and Families.* Washington, DC: GPO, 1991.

Summary of recommendations of the National Commission on Children which was established by Congress as a forum on behalf of the children of the nation.

National Head Start Association. *Head Start, Early Childhood Education, and Day Care: NHSA Overview.* Washington, DC: Author, April 1989.

National Head Start Association. *Head Start: The Nation's Pride, A Nation's Challenge.* Alexandria, VA: NHSA, 1990.

Reports recommendation of the NHSA Silver Ribbon Panel about the vision of Head Start for the 1990s.

National Head Start Association. "Parent Involvement Survey." *NHSA Journal* (Fall 1991): 30–31.

National Head Start Association. *Head Start Income Guidelines Are Out of Touch with Poverty.* Alexandria, VA: NHSA, 1991.

Calls for revising the "official poverty line" or increasing the Head Start guideline to match Medicaid guidelines for young children (133 percent of the poverty line). Currently, Head Start guidelines are lower than those for Medicaid, the Child Care Food Program, WIC, JTPA, food stamps, and the U.S. Department of Housing and Urban Development.

National Institute on Drug Abuse. *A Guide to Mobilizing Ethnic Minority Communities for Drug-Abuse Prevention.* Rockville, MD: U.S. Public Health Service, Alcohol, Drug Abuse, and Mental Health Administration, 1986.

Newsweek. "Everybody Likes Head Start." (February 20, 1989): 49.

Nobles, W., L.L. Goddard, W.E. Cavil, and P.Y. George. *The Culture of Drugs in the Black Community*. Oakland, CA: Black Family Institute, 1987, pp. 10–36.

Omwake, E.B. "Assessment of the Head Start Preschool Education Effort." In Edward Zigler and Jeanette Valentine, eds., *Project Head Start*. New York: Free Press, 1979, pp. 221–230.

Argues that evaluation efforts experienced many problems because of inadequate and constantly shifting funding levels, frequent personnel changes, conflict around goals and approaches, and bureaucratic interference. Explains that by 1970, the preschool program became stronger after a reorganization of the curriculum when IQ change and achievement test scores were not regarded as the primary goal of Head Start. Finds that a pressing problem of the program is short-term training for inexperienced staff.

Orlandi, M.A. *Cultural Competence for Evaluators: A Guide for Alcohol and Other Drug Abuse Prevention Practitioners Working with Ethnic/Racial Communities*. Rockville, MD: HHS/OSAP, 1992.

Identifies the unique characteristics of various cultural groups including Hispanics, African Americans, American Indians, and Asian Americans. Strategies for culturally sensitive evaluations are presented.

Osborne, D., and J. Gaebler. *Reinventing Government: How the Entrepreneurial Spirit Is Transforming the Public Sector from Schoolhouse to Statehouse, City Hall to the Pentagon*. Reading, MA: Addison-Wesley, 1992.

Oyemade, U.J. "The Rationale for Head Start as a Vehicle for Upward Mobility of Minority Families." *American Journal of Orthopsychiatry* (October 1985): 591–602.

Critiques premises that guided the development of the culture-of-poverty theory: the concept of transgenerational poverty, the assumption of education as a vehicle for upward mobility, and the assumption that the child could serve as a vehicle for the economic mobility of the family.

Oyemade, U.J., and D.E. Brandon. *Ecology of Alcohol and Other Drug Use: Helping Black High-Risk Youth.* Rockville, MD: OSAP/ADAMHA/DHHS, 1990.

Presents a comprehensive approach to alcohol and other drug intervention using an integrative, ecological model. Factors addressed include family, culture, environment, media, nutrition, systemic factors, availability, and the pharmaceutical industry. Prevention models based on these issues are presented.

Oyemade, U.J., and V. Washington. "Drug Abuse Prevention Begins in Early Childhood." *Young Children,* 44(9) (1989): 6–12.

Presents an overview of the risk factors associated with the onset of substance abuse. Suggests approaches for primary prevention beginning in preschool.

Oyemade, U.J., and V. Washington. "Family Environment Factors Related to Substance Abuse among High-Risk Youth." In Arlene Stiffman and Larry Davis, eds., *Ethnic Issues in Adolescent Mental Health.* Newbury Park, CA: Sage Publications, 1990, pp. 267–284.

Summarizes research on the association between family factors and substance abuse in black high-risk youth. Results of study of 134 black adolescents in Washington, D.C., revealed that key family values, childrearing practices and other environmental factors differentiated between academic achievers, nonacademic achievers, juvenile delinquents, and teenage parents.

Oyemade, U.J., V. Washington and D.F. Gullo. "The Relationship Between Head Start Parent Involvement and the Economic Self-Sufficiency of Head Start Families." *Journal of Negro Education,* 58(1) (1989): 5–15.

Report of an empirical study of the relationship of the parental involvement component of the Head Start program and the economic and social self-sufficiency of Head Start families and children. Results suggest that

Head Start has had a positive effect on the upward mobility of Head Start parents. A significant number of parents whose children attend high-involvement Head Start centers are economically better off now than they were when their children began Head Start.

Parker, Faith Lamb, Chaya S. Diffkowski, and L. Peay. "Head Start as a Social Support for Mothers: The Psychological Effects of Involvement." *American Journal of Orthopsychiatry* 57 (1987): 220–33.

Studied the psychological effects of Head Start on participating parents. Reports that greater participation resulted in fewer psychological problems, increased feelings of mastery, and greater feelings of fulfillment in life. Discusses the implication of these findings.

Payne, James S., Ruth A. Payne, Cecil D. Mercer, and Roxana G. Davison. *Head Start: A Tragicomedy with Epilogue.* New York: Behavioral Publications, 1973.

Phillips, D. "With a Little Help: Children in Poverty Child Care." In A. Huston, ed., *Children in Poverty: Child Development and Public Policy.* New York: Cambridge University Press, 1992.

Pizzo, Peggy. "Family-Centered Head Start for Infants and Toddlers: A Renewed Direction for Project Head Start." *Young Children* 45 (6) (September 1990): 30–35.

The author reviews characteristics of Head Start programs which addressed infant development from a comprehensive family-centered perspective. Suggests that Head Start launch a national training and technical assistance initiative centered on knowledge exchange about the first three years of life.

Powell, D.R. "Families and Early Childhood Programs." *Research Monographs of the National Association for the Education of Young Children* 3 (1989).

Powell, D.R. *Making It in Today's World: Options for Strengthening Parents' Contributions to Children's Learning.* West Lafayette, IN: Purdue University Department of Child Development and Family Studies, November, 1992.

Studied how parents facilitate their children's learning in both time and community settings, especially what parents think about their children's future and the types of learning environments children are experiencing out of school.

Price-Bonham, S., and P. Skeen. "A Comparison of Black and White Fathers with Implications for Parent Education." *The Family Coordinator*, 28(1) (1979): 53–59.

Primm, B. "Implications of Alcohol and Other Drug Use for Black America." In Oyemade, et al. eds., *The Ecology of Substance Abuse: Helping Black High-Risk Youth*. Washington, DC: HHS/OSAP, 1991.

Prothrow-Stith, D., and M. Weissman. *Deadly Consequences*. New York: Harper Collins, 1991.

Quinton, S.L. and S.A. Johnson. *Identifying the Needs of Drug-Affected Children: Public Policy Issues*. Rockville, MD: HHS/OSAP, 1992.

Summarizes research related to the effects of prenatal exposure to alcohol and other drugs. Discusses the impact of the social environment on development. Makes recommendation regarding strategies for responding by the child welfare system and other programs.

Raver, Cybele C., and Edward F. Zigler. "Three Steps Forward, Two Steps Back. Head Start and the Measurement of Social Competence." *Young Children* 46(4) (1991): 3–8.

Points out that present evaluation measures and curriculum measures being advocated by the Head Start central administration are narrowly cognitive in orientation. Recommends that Head Start concern for the whole person be reflected in the valuative measures and curricula used by Head Start. Claims that Head Start has earned recognition as a highly successful program. However, based on evaluation experience it is certain that Head Start does not significantly raise IQ scores. Future evaluators would be forced to focus on this domain if a cognitive curriculum and evaluative tools are adopted.

Resnik, H., S.E. Gardner, R.P. Lorion, and C.E. Marcus. *Youth and Drugs: Society's Mixed Messages.* Rockville, MD: HHS/OSAP, 1990.

Analyzes the role of mass media and communications in the use of drugs in the U.S. Suggests strategies for addressing this problem.

Reynolds, A.J. *Effects of a preschool plus follow-on intervention program for children at risk.* Paper presented at the biennial meeting of the Society for Research in Child Development, New Orleans, March 1993.

Richmond, Julius R., Deborah J. Stipek, and Edward Zigler. "A Decade of Head Start." In Edward Zigler and Jeanette Valentine, eds., *Project Head Start.* New York: Free Press, 1979, pp. 135–152.

Shows how Head Start, an effort of several groups, was organized to help the nation's disadvantaged children and their families. Discusses the goals and components of Head Start, Head Start's mandate and funding, and innovative Head Start demonstration programs. Tries to clear up misconceptions about Head Start, and offers a candid evaluation.

Robinson, James L., and Willa Bartie Choper. "Another Perspective on Program Evaluation: The Parents Speak. In Edward Zigler and Jeanette Valentine, eds., *Project Head Start.* New York: Free Press, 1979, pp. 467–479.

Assesses parents' contribution to the Head Start program. Finds that parents are proud of the changes made to their lives though the program. Discusses some of the benefits of the program, such as gains in cognitive development, improved health, and the positive attitude of parents toward their children.

Roman, Virginia. "Statement for the Record." *Oversight Hearing of the Head Start Program, Subcommittee on Human Resources of the Committee on Education and Labor, House of*

Representatives. Washington, DC: U.S. Government Printing Office, February 23, 1982, pp. 76–78.

Rosario, Jose, and John M. Love. *Evaluations of Bilingual Programs: Examples of the Reproductive Functions of Evaluative Research, Bilingual Education Paper Series. Volume 4. No. 7.* Los Angeles: California State University, April 1979.

Contrasts examples of bilingual research and describes the Head Start strategy for Spanish-speaking children.

Ross, Catherine J. "Early Skirmishes with Poverty: The Historical Roots of Head Start." In Edward Zigler and Jeanette Valentine, eds., *Project Head Start: A Legacy of the War on Poverty.* New York: Free Press, 1979, pp. 21–42.

Looks at the development of formal education in the U.S. from the early 1800s through the 1900s. Discusses the care of indigent children, kindergartens, and pre-school health programs. Examines the early involvement of the federal government in day care programs in the 1930s. Shows how this led to more government involvement, thus giving birth to Project Head Start.

Royster, E.C., J.C. Laxson, T. Fer, S. Fosburg, M. Nauta, B. Nelson, and G. Takata. *A National Survey: Head Start Graduates and Their Peers.* Cambridge, MA: Abt Associates. (Report No. AAI–77–54, 1978)

Ryan, Sally, ed. *A Report on Longitudinal Evaluations of Preschool Programs, Vol. 1.* Washington, DC: HEW. (Publication No. [OHD] 74–24, 1974)

Attempts to assess the impact of preschool intervention programs by reviewing the findings of small, controlled long-term evaluations of programs in various parts of the U.S. Eight researchers with available longitudinal data contributed to this volume. All of the articles report an immediate impact of preschool intervention on a short-term basis.

Scholars' Letter to Congress, March 16, 1993.

A letter signed by sixteen scientists and sent to members of Congress in support of Project Head Start. The letter endorsed President Clinton's proposal "to strengthen and fully fund Head Start," and "to make the resources available to strengthen the quality of Head Start."

Schorr, L.B. *Within Our Reach: Breaking the Cycle of Disadvantage.* New York: Doubleday, 1988.

Schweinhart, L.J., and D.P. Weikart. *Young Children Grow Up: The Effects of the Perry Preschool Program on Youths Through Age Fifteen.* Ypsilanti, MI.: High/Scope Educational Research Foundation, 1980.

Schweinhart, L.J., and David P. Weikart. "What Do We Know So Far? Do Head Start Programs Work?" *High Scope Resource Magazine* 5 (Winter 1986): 1, 20, 22–23.

Critiques the report of the Head Start Evaluation, Synthesis, and Utilization Project by CSR, Inc. (see McKey et al., 1985). The authors argue that this report draws conclusions without adequate evidence, fails to consider all of the relevant evidence available, over-generalizes the findings of studies, and fails to distinguish between low quality of design and high quality of design studies.

Schweinhart, L. and D. Weikart. *Significant Benefits: The High/Scope Perry Preschool Study Through Age Twenty-seven.* Ypsilanti, MI: Author, 1993.

Presents longitudinal results of a preschool enrichment program for 123 poor black children through age twenty-seven. The major findings were: over the lifetimes of the participants, the preschool program returns to the public an estimated $7.16 for every dollar invested; that project participants had higher rates of home ownership, levels of schooling completed, a lower percentage receiving social services, and fewer arrests.

Schweinhart, L.J., D.P. Weikart, and M.B. Larner. "Consequences of Three Preschool Curriculum Models through Age Fifteen." *Early Childhood Research Quarterly* 1 (1) (1986): 15–45.

Shipman, V.C. *Disadvantaged Children and Their First School Experiences: Demographic Indexes of Socioeconomic Status and Maternal Behaviors on Attitudes.* Princeton, NJ: Educational Testing Service, 1972. (ERIC ED069424)

Shure, M.B. "Social Competence as a Problem-Solving Skill." In J.D. Wine and M.D. Smye, eds., *Social Competence.* New York: Guilford Press, 1981.

Shure, M.B. and G. Spivak. *Problem-Solving Techniques in Childrearing.* San Francisco: Jossey-Bass, 1978.

Sigel, I.E. "Preschool Education: For Whom and Why?" *New Directions for Child Development* 53 (1991): 83–91.

Skerry, Peter. "The Charmed Life of Head Start." *Public Interest* 73 (1983): 18–40.

Reviews a series of challenges that Head Start has weathered that fosters the claim that Head Start has had a "charmed" existence. Skerry argues that one reason Head Start has endured is because it has managed to be many things to many constituencies including a compensatory education program, a provider of health services, and a catalyst for community change. While Head Start has never lived up to its original claims, Head Start has been able to deliver something to just about everyone.

Slaughter, Diana T. "What Is the Future of Head Start?" *Young Children* (March 1982): 3–9.

Argues that Head Start has accomplished everything but what it was originally expected to accomplish: equal educational opportunity. As a primary prevention program, Head Start's accomplishments surpass the limited, rather naive, early expectations. Head Start instigated some crucial dialogues between people of highly diverse social backgrounds who cared about poor children.

Slaughter, Diana T., ed. *Black Children and Poverty: A Developmental Perspective.* San Francisco: Jossey-Bass, 1988.

Presents developmental perspectives on black children and poverty. Includes contemporary perspectives on socialization and development and impact of black children on research and social policy.

Slaughter, Diana T., Rachel W. Lindsay, K. Nakagawa, and U.S. Kuehne. "Who Gets Involved? Head Start Mothers as Persons." *The Journal of Negro Education* 58 (1) (1989): 5–15.

Presents results of study which designates specific parent program activities within the five Head Start aims for its parental involvement components that parents identify as beneficial. Results also suggest that intensity of involvement is correlated with maternal personality development.

Slaughter, Diana T., Valora Washington, Ura Jean Oyemade, and Rachel W. Lindsay. "Head Start: A Backward and Forward Look." *SRCD Social Policy Report* 3 (2) (Summer 1988).

Presents an overview of the history of Head Start particularly in terms of parental involvement, cultural diversity, and responses to the changing needs of families. Suggests that resolution of these issues is critical for the issue of service to low-income, ethnic minority children.

Slaughter-Defoe, Diana T., K. Nakagawa, R. Takauishi, and D.J. Johnson. "Toward Cultural/Ecological Perspectives on Schooling and Achievement in African- and Asian-American Children." *Child Development* 61 (2) (1990): 363.

Slavin, R.E., N.A. Madden, L.J.,Dolan, B.A.,Wasik, S. Ross, and L. Smith. *"Whenever and Wherever We Choose. . .": The Replication of Success for All.* Paper presented at the annual meeting of the American Educational Research Association, Atlanta, GA: April 1993.

Slavin, R.E., N.A. Madden, N.L. Karweit, L. Dolan, and B.A. Wasik. *Success for All: A Relentless Approach to Prevention and Early Intervention in Elementary Schools.* Arlington, VA: Educational Research Service, 1992.

Smart, R.G., and D. Fejer. "Drug Use among Adolescents and Their Parents: Using the Generation Gap in Mood

Modification." *Journal of Abnormal Psychology* 70 (1972): 153–166.

Smith, Marshall, and Joan S. Bissell. "Report Analysis: The Impact of Head Start." *Harvard Educational Review* 49 (February 1970): 51–104.

Smith, S. "Two-generational Program Models: A New Intervention Strategy." *Social Policy Report* 5 (Spring 1991). Society for Research in Child Development.

Smith, S., S. Blank, and J.T. Bond. *One Program, Two Generations: A Report on the Forum on Children and the Family Support Act*. New York: Foundation for Child Development, 1990.

Smith, S., S. Blank, and R. Collins. *Pathways to Self-Sufficiency for Two Generations: Designing Welfare-to-Work Programs that Benefit Children and Strengthen Families*. New York: Foundation for Child Development, 1992.

The goal of improving the economic, physical, and psychological well-being of children is usually approached indirectly through the benefits that accrue to children from their parent's improved economic situation and new self-esteem gained from employment. This text argues for a more direct approach: a two-generation family-centered strategy in which parenting education and support services provided directly to children should be added components of work/welfare programs. The linkage of JOBS programs with Head Start family service centers and comprehensive child development programs is already taking place in Kentucky, Philadelphia, and several other sites around the country.

Spivak, G., and M.B. Shure. *Social Adjustment of Young Children*. San Francisco: Jossey-Bass, 1974.

Spivak, G., and M.B. Shure. *Problem-solving Techniques in Childrearing*. San Francisco: Jossey-Bass, 1978.

Steiner, Gilbert Y. *The Children's Cause*. Washington, DC: The Brookings Institution, 1976.

Examines the apparatus for making children's policy, and evaluates policy proposals against the background of tension between proponents of public, rather than private, responsibility. Contends that the divisiveness of public relief politics is largely attributable to the growth in the number and cost of dependent children.

Stephan, S. *Head Start Issues in FY 1986: Funding, Administration, and Recent Evaluations.* Washington, DC: Congressional Research Service, January 15, 1986.

Reviews the background of Project Head Start including federal administration issues, local administration issues, and program evaluation reports.

Stewart, G. *Head Start: Percentage of Eligible Children Served and Recent Expansions.* Washington, DC: Congressional Research Service, July 30, 1991. (#91-572)

Estimates that Head Start reaches 28 percent of the 2,044,200 children eligible by law and regulation.

Stipek, D.J, Jeanette Valentine, and E. Zigler. "Project Head Start: A Critique of Theory and Practice." In Edward Zigler and Jeanette Valentine, eds., *Project Head Start: A Legacy of the War on Poverty.* New York: Free Press, 1979, pp. 477–494.

Appraises the theories behind Head Start and the problems encountered in their implementation.

Subcommittee on Human Resources of the Committee on Education and Labor, House of Representatives. *Oversight Hearing on the Head Start Program.* Washington, DC: U.S. Government Printing Office, February 23, 1982.

Subcommittee of Human Resources of the Committee on Education and Labor, House of Representatives. *Authorizations for Head Start, Follow Through, Community Services, and Establish Child Care Information and Referral Services.* Washington, DC: U.S. Government Printing Office, March 21, 1984.

Thacker, S.B., D.G. Addis, R.A. Goodman et al. "Infectious Diseases and Injuries in Child Daycare: Opportunities for Healthier Children." *Journal of the American Medical Association* 268 (1992): 1720–1726.

U.S. Department of Education, National Center for Research Statistics. *Profile of Preschool Children's Child Care and Early Education Program Participation.* Washington, DC: U.S. Department of Education, 1993.

U.S. Department of Health, Education, and Welfare. *The Status of Handicapped Children in Head Start Programs: Seventh Annual Report of the U.S. Department of Health, Education, and Welfare to the Congress of the United States on Services Provided to Handicapped Children in Project Head Start.* Washington, DC: HEW, February 1980.

U.S. Department of Health, Education, and Welfare, Office of Child Development, *Recommendations for a Head Start Program by a Panel of Experts,* Washington, DC: HEW/OCD, February 19, 1965. p. 4. (Now available from the Administration on Children, Youth, and Families, Office of Human Development, Department of Health and Human Services, Washington, DC.)

U.S. Department of Health and Human Services, Administration on Children, Youth, and Families, Department of Health and Human Services. *The Commissioner's Advisory Panel on Research and Evaluation: Implementing the Blueprint Interim Report.* Washington, DC: Author, March 1993.

This report contains the recommendations of the panel's first task: identifying needed studies that should be undertaken in the years ahead. These recommendations were based on the identification of gaps in the Head Start knowledge base. The panel also deliberated the parameters for the design and conduct of such studies.

U.S. Department of Health and Human Services, Administration on Children, Youth, and Families, Head Start Bureau. *Head Start Research and Evaluation: A Blueprint for the Future.* Washington, DC: Author, September 1990. (DHHS Publication No. ACY91-31195)

Presents the key findings and recommendations for the advisory panel for the Head Start Evaluation Design

Project. The multiracial panel of national experts represented the first opportunity in fifteen years for a systematic analysis of research needs relevant to the future of Head Start. The report presents: 1) eight recommendations for an overall strategy and general principles; 2) four recommended research directions needed for building a future knowledge base; and 3) four research support activities needed to create an infrastructure for Head Start research and evaluation.

U.S. Department of Health and Human Services. *Head Start Expansion: Grantee Experiences.* Washington, DC: U.S. Government Printing Office, 1993. (DHSS Publication No. OEI-00-91-00760)

Summary of the evaluation of Head Start by the Inspector General in 1993. Findings with regard to enrollment, facilities, staffing, transportation, social services and planning are presented. Recommendations for improvement are included.

U.S. Department of Health and Human Services. *Parent Training Is Prevention: Preventing Alcohol and Other Drug Problems Among Youth in the Family.* Rockville, MD: HHS/OSAP, 1991. (DHHS Publication No. ADM 91-1715)

A guide to help communities identify and implement programs designed specifically for parents. Presents basic information on prevention, parenting, and the roles that parents play in raising children who are alcohol and drug free. Highlights ethnic and cultural consider-ations and concludes with guidelines for program implementation.

U.S. Department of Health and Human Services. *Breaking New Ground for American Indian and Alaska Native Youth: Program Summaries.* Rockville, MD: HHS/OSAP, 1990. (DHHS Publication No. ADM 90–1705)

Reviews the incidence of AOD abuse in the American Indian community. Includes a detailed review of the literature including the historical context. Presents an overview of the different types of AOD prevention programs in American Indian communities.

U.S. Department of Health and Human Services. *Proceedings of a National Conference on Preventing Alcohol and Drug Abuse in Black Communities.* Rockville, MD: HHS/OSAP, 1990. (DHHS Publication No. ADM 89-1648)

Presents the proceedings of the National Conference on Preventing AOD Abuse in the Black Community. Issues addressed include prevention models for the black community, networking, community resources such as churches, family and other factors.

U.S. Department of Health and Human Services. *Evaluating Head Start Expansion Through Performance Indicators.* Washington, D.C.: U.S. Government Printing Office, 1993. (DHSS Publication No. OEI-09-91-00762)

Summary of the evaluation of Head Start expansion by the Inspector General in 1993. No difference in grantee performance as a result of expansion was found. Deficiencies and recommendations for corrective action are included.

U.S. Department of Health and Human Services. *Promoting Family Literacy Through Head Start.* Washington, DC: U.S. Government Printing Office, 1990. (DHHS Publication No. ACF 91-31266)

Provides an overview of the problem of intergenerational illiteracy and suggests methods of incorporating family literacy promotion into Head Start functions. Describes existing family literacy efforts and lists available resources for use in Head Start programs.

U.S. Department of Health and Human Services. *Head Start in the 1980s: A Report Requested by the President of the United States.* Washington, DC: September 1980.

U.S. Department of Health and Human Services, Office of the Inspector General. *Dysfunctional Families in the Head Start Program: Meeting the Challenge.* Washington, DC: Author, 1989A.

U.S. Department of Health and Human Services, Office of the Inspector General. *Final Report: Commissioner's Task Force on Social Services in Head Start.* Washington, DC: Author, 1989B.

U.S. Department of Health and Human Services, Office of Human Development Services, Administration on Children, Youth, and Families, Head Start Bureau. *Head Start Program Performance Standards (45-CFR 1304).* Washington, DC: HHS, November 1984B. (Publication No. [OHDS] 84-31131)

Sets out the goals of Project Head Start as they may be achieved by the program components, with emphasis on the performance standards.

U.S. Department of Health and Human Services. *Project Head Start Statistical Fact Sheet.* Washington, DC: HHS, December 1985, and January 1987, 1993.

Lists a number of facts about Head Start: budget, number of programs, enrollment, racial/ethnic composition, ages of children, location of sites, number of sites, cost per child, number of staff, number of volunteers, and other information.

U.S. Public Health Service. *Drug Abuse and Drug Abuse Research: The Third Triennial Report to the Congress from the Secretary.* Washington, DC: HHS, 1991A. (Publication Number ADM 91-1704)

U.S. Public Health Service. *Healthy People 2000. National Health Promotion and Disease Prevention Objectives.* Washington, DC: HHS, 1991B. (Publication Number PHS-91-1704)

Valentine, Jeanette. "Program Development in Head Start: A Multifaceted Approach to Meeting the Needs of Families and Children." In Edward Zigler and Jeanette Valentine, eds., *Project Head Start: A Legacy of the War on Poverty.* New York: Free Press, 1979, pp. 349–366.

Reports that Head Start has experimented with a number of approaches to meet the needs of children and families in poverty. Discusses comprehensive services to families and children, health service delivery demonstrations, and special programs for target groups as part of a review of programs tried over the years. Examines the coordination of Head Start with other agencies serving disadvantaged children and looks at directions for the future.

Valentine, Jeanette, C.J. Ross, and E. Zigler. "Epilogue." *Project Head Start.* New York: Free Press, 1979, pp. 509–516.

Gives an overview of the Head Start program. Looks at the problems it has had to overcome and the successes it has had. Argues that the involvement of parents may, in the long run, be more important than the children's performance. Sees the present status of the program as a national laboratory that offers a combination of educational, health, and social welfare services to the nation's children. Looks to the future and concludes that the flexible nature of the program should allow it to adopt to change in the future.

Valentine, Jeanette, and Evan Stark. "The Social Context of Parent Involvement in Head Start." In Edward Zigler and Jeanette Valentine, eds., *Project Head Start.* New York: Free Press, 1979, pp. 291–314.

Contends that there were conflicting ideas on parent involvement in Head Start—some saw parents as participating in education programs while others saw parents as decision makers. Describes four dimensions of parent involvement as set out by Head Start: 1) making decisions about programs; 2) volunteering; 3) planning parent education; and 4) receiving home visits from Head Start staff.

Washington, Valora. "Historical and Contemporary Linkages Between Black Child Development and Social Policy." In Diana T. Slaughter, ed., *Black Children and Poverty: A Developmental Perspective.* San Francisco: Jossey-Bass, 1988.

Washington, Valora, and Ura Jean Oyemade. "Changing Family Trends; Head Start Must Respond." *Young Children* (September 1985): 12–19.

Discusses the impact of four family trends on Project Head Start: the feminization of poverty, the rise in teen parenting, the surge in the number of mothers of preschool children in the work force, and the increasing challenge to poor families to attain economic self-sufficiency. Recommendations are offered as to how Head Start can better serve children and families affected by these trends. This article served as the basis for this book.

Washington, Valora. "Head Start: How Appropriate for Minority Families in the 1980s?" *American Journal of Orthopsychiatry* 55 (October 1985A): 557–591.

Questions Head Start's continuing relevance for minority children and their families. Argues that the challenge of Head Start in the 1980s is to maintain, advocate for, and monitor program quality.

Washington, Valora, and Ura Jean Oyemade. *Project Head Start: Past, Present, and Future Trends in the Context of Family Needs.* New York and London: Garland, 1987.

Watson, B.H. *Young Unwed Fathers Pilot Project. Initial Implementation Report.* Philadelphia: Public/Private Ventures, Fall 1992.

Weikart, D.P. *Quality Preschool Programs: A Long-Term Social Investment.* New York: Ford, 1989.

Weikart, D.P., and L.J. Schweinhart. "Disadvantaged Children and Curriculum Effects." *New Directions for Child Development* 53 (1991): 57–64.

Weiner, T. "Senate Unit Calls U.S. Most Violent Country on Earth." *The Boston Globe* (March 13, 1991).

The U.S. leads the industrialized world in homicides, rapes, and assaults.

Weisberg, H.I., and W. Haney. *Longitudinal Evaluation of Head Start Planned Variation and Follow Through.* Cambridge, MA: Huron Institute, 1977.

Weissbourd, R. *Making the System Work for Poor Children.* Cambridge, MA: Harvard University Press, 1991.

Westinghouse Learning Corporation. *The Impact of Head Start: An Evaluation of the Effects of Head Start on Children's Cognitive and Affective Development. Volumes I-H and Executive Summary.* Athens, OH: Ohio University, 1969.

White, K.R., M.J. Taylor, and V.D. Moss. "Does Research Support Claims about the Benefits of Involving Parents in Early Intervention Programs?" *Review of Educational Research* 62 (1992): 91–125.

Whitebook, M., C. Howes, and D. Phillips. *Who Cares? Child Care Teachers and the Quality of Care in America.* Oakland, CA: Child Care Employees Project, 1989.

Zero to Three. Can They Hope to Feel Safe Again? Impact of Community Violence on Infants, Toddlers, Their Parents, and Practitioners. Arlington, VA: *Zero to Three,* National Center for Clinical Infant Programs, 1992.

Zigler, E. "Assessing Head Start at Twenty: An Invited Commentary." *American Journal of Orthopsychiatry* 55 (October 1985): 603–609.

Critiques articles by Valora Washington (1985A) and Ura Jean Oyemade (1985). Highlights the accomplishments of Head Start over two decades as well as some of its limitations.

Zigler, E. "Project Head Start: Success or Failure?" In E. Zigler and J. Valentine, eds., *Project Head Start.* New York: Free Press, 1979, pp. 495–507.

Examines the different objectives of Project Head Start—social competence, health, intellectual ability, social and emotional development, family involvement, and community change in reference to the disadvantaged child. Discusses elements which lead to an overly cognitive emphasis in evaluations of Head Start and other remedial programs. Argues that the broad-based goals of Project Head Start make it a success.

Zigler, E., W. Abelson, and V. Seitz. "Motivational Factors in the Performance of Economically Disadvantaged Children on the Peabody Picture Vocabulary Test." *Child Development* 44 (1973): 294–303.

Zigler, E., and Karen Anderson. "An Idea Whose Time Had Come: The Intellectual and Political Climate for Head Start." In Edward Zigler and Jeanette Valentine, eds., *Project Head Start.* New York: The Free Press, 1979, pp. 3–19.

Zigler, E., and Mary E. Lang. "Head Start: Looking Toward the Future." *Young Children* 38(1983): 3–6.

Examines the strengths and accomplishments of the Head Start program and suggests directions for future program development. Stresses the need for attention to program quality, staff-child ratios, class size, and teacher salaries and benefits.

Zigler, E., and S. Muenchow. *Head Start: The Inside Story of America's Most Successful Educational Experiment.* New York: Basic Books, 1992.

Gives an historical account of Head Start and makes recommendations for future Head Start programs. Chronicles how two Republican administrations tried to short-change, if not dismantle, Head Start, while another Republican became one of the program's greatest protectors. Proposes that parent involvement and comprehensive services have been the key to Head Start success.

Zigler, E., and Leslie Rescorla. "Social Science and Social Policy: The Case of Social Competence as a Goal of Intervention Programs." In Richard A. Kassochau, Lyn P. Rehmm, and Leonard P. Ullmann, eds., *Psychology Research, Public Policy and Practice: Toward a Productive Partnership.* New York: Praeger, 1985, pp. 62–94.

Presents the case of social competence as the appropriate goal for early intervention programs and describes the authors' efforts to conceptualize and operationalize the concept of social competence.

Zigler, E. and Sally J. Styfco, eds. *Head Start and Beyond. A National Plan for Extended Childhood Intervention.* New Haven, CT: Yale University Press, 1993.

Evaluates existing Head Start programs and presents proposals for maximizing their effectiveness.

Zigler, E., and Jeanette Valentine, eds. *Project Head Start: A Legacy of the War on Poverty*. New York: Free Press, 1979.

Subject Index

Index of Names and Authors